# Gun-Totin' Chaplain

### Jerry Autry

AIRBORNE PRESS
SAN FRANCISCO · PSF

All quotations are credited if possible. In those cases where they are not, we would like to, and if a reader will let us know, in future editions we will do so. Special appreciation goes to Don Stevenson and John Kampschroeder for sharing their Vietnam pictures and to the following Web sites: LZSally.com, *Allserve*.blogspot.com, and Scr eamingeaglesthroughtime.com.

Cover and book design by Sue Knopf.

Library of Congress Cataloging-in-Publication Data

Autry, Jerry, 1939-
  Gun totin' chaplain / by Jerry Autry.
    p. cm.
  ISBN 0-934145-11-3 (alk. paper)
  1. Autry, Jerry, 1939- 2. United States. Army--Chaplains--Biography.
3. Chaplains, Military--United States--Biography. 4. Vietnam War, 1961-1975--Chaplains--Biography. 5. Vietnam War, 1961-1975--Personal narratives, American. I. Title. II. Title: Gun toting chaplain.

  UG626.2.A98A3 2006
  959.704'37--dc22
  [B]
                                                    2006029673

Printed in the United States of America

Airborne Press
Presidio 29464
San Francisco, CA 94129

*To Jackie, the epitome of the wonderful military wife:*
*long-suffering, dedicated, patient, committed,*
*sacrificing, patriotic, unwavering. The best.*
*For all those missed dinners, the times when*
*you needed me most, and I was gone.*
*What can I say other than a big-time inadequate thanks.*

# Contents

# Acknowledgments

Writing about one's experiences is an interesting process, to say the least. For me, sometimes it has been insightful, always painful. For a self-diagnosed ADD (attention deficit disorder) type, remaining focused on the task is difficult almost beyond description. I've read all the ADD books, so I "get it." Once I've finished something, if only in my mind, I'm ready to move on to the next project. But writing *Gun Totin' Chaplain*, though written in my mind, was not down on paper—so I had to say, "Just do it."

Along the way, I've had enormous encouragement. For a long time nobody wanted to hear about Vietnam, but during the most recent presidential campaign, Vietnam took center stage, and not always for the best reasons. Vietnam was our first truly mismanaged war any way you look at it. Telling my story—as one of millions—at times seemed a little superfluous, but a few people wanted to hear it. My friends asked, and members of my former church, where I preached for eight years, quizzed me from time to time, since they often heard my stories from the pulpit. In the congregation, we had great World War II heroes who were a constant inspiration. We discovered—

after they had transitioned from this life into the next—that a couple of them were true war heroes. One had won a silver star while serving in the Navy during the Korean war. My suspicion is that he had been a Navy Seal and had never told anyone. Another had been a POW briefly and organized a local Philippine resistance movement. He was a celebrated sniper and had won many awards. His family never knew about any of this. "Maybe I just should write my memoirs," I thought.

When I retired, my casual buddies went from casuals to regulars, and they encouraged me to write. My wife calls them my "girlfriends." Michael, Gary, Ray, Andy, Larry, and a few straphangers (airborne term for those who show up occasionally)—Dave, Leonard, Saul, Lee, Greg, Tom, Javier, Tracy. Michael stayed on me mercilessly once the memoirs were written to get them out to the public. "Needs to be read," he said. I pressed on. I posted them on the Airborne Press Web site just to get relief from his relentless badgering. One day we were out running, and he said something that convinced me to publish. "You are the least ego-driven person I know, but sometimes you have to think of the greater good, and the greater good is to tell your story. You have something to say." I was humbled. Add to this the comment of another friend: "You should publish your memoirs for all those Vietnam vets who are not here to do their own."

Thanks to Ruth Lukkari, who entrusted me with the story of her brother's death in Vietnam and the effect it had upon her family. I was inspired.

Thanks to the Airborne Press webzine for the forum to spout off my musings, ramblings, and drivel over the years. My niece Kathryn goes beyond expectations for the way she takes my ADD thoughts and translates them into sometimes readable and understandable postings. My good friend and editor, Ellen Stevenson, is without peer. She has cleaned up my stuff in so many ways. Her husband, Don, and I were in Vietnam together and he's one of my heroes. Now a judge, his commitment to Vietnam vets constantly inspires me.

There are so many more I could thank, and I know I've left out key persons. Please, please forgive me and know I'm grateful.

The "girlfriends": Larry, Ray, Jerry, Michael, Andy, and Gary.

# Preface

Writing about Vietnam while the Iraq War is going on has been excruciating. Day by day, as I sat, watched, read—it was Vietnam revisited. After I retired and became a church pastor, I produced a little newsletter as part of our weekly bulletin. It was mainly thoughts—things I had garnished from various sources—and then 9/11 happened, and like many Americans, I was in a continuous state of grief. My weekly diatribe became more and more my inner thoughts.

Then Iraq became a war and, thankfully for all concerned, especially my wonderful little church, I retired before they ran me off (this is really a joke as they would have, unfortunately, put up with me). I became what I considered a constructive critic of the war. I support the soldiers, as do most Americans. We learned our lessons, and this fact alone may be the lasting legacy of Vietnam if there is one—the soldier is just doing his job. I grimaced constantly with the mismanagement of the war from day one. When the war began, my feeling was that we had to get Saddam either now or later. I preferred later but gave the powers that be the benefit of the doubt. Like many Americans, my optimism soon vanished. After having experienced Vietnam, the very idea that we would have such a debacle again was unfathomable. Not only were we mismanaging it but worse: we violated every single lesson we learned from Vietnam. Worse still, the same as Vietnam, we let politics intrude, and it all went to hell. Brave Americans were fighting and dying, and the politicians were rearranging the deck chairs on the *Titanic*.

Day by day, it appeared to get worse. I debated constantly with my friends about a government that seemed to be in total denial. Would we ever learn? No. Because of all this, I decided to intersperse my own thoughts and writings that I'd done for the Airborne Press webzine about Iraq in the middle of my Vietnam story. I didn't know how this would play out with those who had been so kind as to read the rough draft, but it was very cathartic for me. In the end, we decided it would work better to make my musings into observations rather than incorporate them within chapters. There was some repetition, as I couldn't avoid it in commenting about the same subject. And my great passion about universal service kept forcing me to sing about it like a broken record. Sorry.

Several of my chaplain buddies have written books about Vietnam, and I've read them all. They're good. Mine may be a little more philosophical. I've tried to convey the contributions chaplains make in war and peace. Few people have a clue as to just how pivotal a chaplain's role is. He or she can be an unsung hero. The bright spot in the Iraq war, if there is one, is the good work the chaplains are doing, for the soldiers and, no doubt, for the Iraqis.

This book has been an intensely laborious endeavor. It's the second time I've attempted to write my Vietnam memoirs. The first was when I was a student at the Command and General Staff College and Vietnam fell. It was one of the worst days of my life, as I had to admit that Vietnam had been a waste. When the Iraq war began, it became evident to me that it was going to be an IRAQNAM—as mismanaged as Vietnam had been or worse. I desperately needed a vehicle to express my frustrations and anger.

Someone once said that if you write something you feel strongly about, you should be willing to promote it. This is very hard for me as I'm slightly reclusive and because I'm ADD. I owe my buddy Michael beaucoup credit for badgering me unmercifully to get it published.

A memoir is really about an experience: in some wonderful way, putting memories on paper, interspersed with not a little speculation. Part of the difficulty is wondering whether what I am saying is truth or opinion. Someone once said, "All writing is invention," meaning, I guess, that it comes out of someone's head.

What I have is some raw material, and I'm trying to piece together my story. In some ways, it is my own growth path. I want to share the truth. Sometimes I have had to ask, "What is the truth?" My recollection and the recollection of my Vietnam buddies do not always mesh. Who is right? Or is there a right? Most of the time, I've chosen to go their way. In general the stories and facts are the same, but details are often different. I don't think that anybody is more on top of wanting the facts than a

Vietnam combat vet. To give an example of the mud and mire, I met a vet who was with another unit who said he was attached to our unit for a bit. I don't remember him, but some do, and it appears that he has constructed an entire scenario around the time he says he was with my unit. Is this untrue; true? I simply don't know and don't know whether it matters.

Truth is not relative. We're not talking about such notions as recently we've seen with memoirs when much of what was said was made up even if the general story was true. We are talking almost forty years ago, and the memories at best are slightly worn. As one of my buddies said, it is somewhat like a vinyl record that is worn and may skip a bit.

For me, this is my story and how it was.

# Prologue

I had been in Vietnam for three weeks, but it already seemed like forever. I was riding with the brigade chaplain and a driver in a jeep to my first assignment at LZ (landing zone) Sally. Strange. We were in a foreign country riding through fields of farmers up to their hips in rice paddies. I sure wasn't in North Carolina anymore.

We slowed to a stop. "Are we there?" I said to the brigade chaplain. "Naw, looks like the bridge is out and we've got to go around." Another jeep was ahead of us and it made sense for us to just go around them and let their jeep follow us. But we didn't—the jeep ahead backed up and started across the ditch beside the bridge. The next thing I knew there was a horrendous explosion. In what looked and felt like slow motion, the other jeep was picked up and thrown into the air. It turned over and those inside tumbled out. Someone screamed. Then there was shocked silence. We collected ourselves and realized that the jeep had been blown up. Instinctively, I ran to the demolished jeep, which was not all that smart. It had been blown into three or four pieces—the carnage was unreal. I saw a soldier's left arm, which was severed from his body, and his left leg was shredded up to the thigh. There was no doubt he was dead. The brigade chaplain's face was ashen, and he said, over and over, "Oh, Jesus." As I think about it now, that was a very appropriate comment.

This was my first introduction to the VC (Vietcong). They had booby-trapped the makeshift path for vehicles at the side of the bridge. Two people were dead—the driver of the jeep and a PFC riding with him. A helicopter appeared carrying the medics.

"They're all your enemies," a sergeant told me when I first came into the country. Maybe they are, I thought, as I looked at medics putting the remains of a soldier into a rubber bag. I felt sick.

Two questions raged in my head: *What have I gotten myself into? How did I get here?*

*It is well war is so terrible;*
*otherwise, we would love it too much.*

GENERAL ROBERT E. LEE, LOOKING OVER THE CARNAGE
OF THE CIVIL WAR BATTLE FOR FREDRICKSBURG, VIRGINIA

# I Want to Go to Vietnam—
# I Want to Kill Some Vietcong

(sung in cadence over and over, running and training)

The plane leveled out at 25,000 feet. I was sitting over the wing. The plane was a Flying Tiger. It was 1968. When we walked out to the runway to board it, I, like most of the guys, was in a daze. I remember looking at the tail of the plane—dark blue with "Flying Tigers" written parallel to the slope of the tail and then an American flag at the top. At the time I thought, *Pretty impressive.* The rest of the plane was light blue and had a metallic look with two stripes painted horizontally in the middle, wide red and dark blue. Funny what you remember. Flying Tigers. This was a cargo plane, but it could be used for charter. That was the best thing we'd be called for a long time—*charter.*

The silence was thick, each of us lost in his own thoughts. In just a few hours we'd touch down at Bien Hoa Air Base. Most on our flight were *cherries,* a term I'd learned at Travis Air Force Base. I can't tell you the number of times I ran into people who'd say, "Going to 'Nam? A cherry, eh?" Everybody has to start somewhere—to be a cherry at some time. The vets were easy to spot. Hanging down from their left pockets were brightly colored unit badges: the four clovers of the 4th Infantry Division, the castle and sword of the Military Assistance Command, and the Screaming Eagle of the 101st Airborne Division. All pointed poignantly to the 400,000 plus Americans in Vietnam. The vets seemed very mellow and resigned. In their eyes I could see that proverbial thousand-yard stare.

I can still remember the pilot saying, "We'll be landing in about twenty-five minutes. Presently, we're starting our descent, and you'll deplane at Bien Hoa Air Base. We hope you've enjoyed your flight and that your stay in Vietnam will be a pleasant and safe one." *Oh, yeah—it's going to be pleasant, all right.* His voice trailed off at the end. I guess there wasn't much more the guy could say. We were all pretty quiet. A few more minutes and all our wondering and doubts would be realized. For at least the last couple of years, I'd read and been conscious of the Vietnam war on TV, and now I was part of it. I wondered what life would be like when my year was up. My insides were churning.

The first thing you notice when you get off the plane in Vietnam is the heat and the sweaty palms. I'm from North Carolina, and I know heat. Unless you're from the South, it might be a new feeling. At Fort Bragg in particular, July and August equal hot and sweaty. If you get out of your car, before you're back in, you're drenched. Bragg is not a good place to be if you don't like sweat. I used to laugh and tell guys that sweat in North Carolina is an aphrodisiac—not sure I could sell the aphrodisiac thing in the Nam.

I wondered about my unit. I wanted to be with the airborne, Special Forces preferably. Why? I had trained for it—just about killed myself jumping out of a plane over the Uharrie Forest with an M60 machine gun. After I landed, I remember lying there thinking to myself, "I know that I have broken something." No one could hit the ground at 30 miles an hour and not break a bone. There was no feeling in any part of me. I began to move my hands along my body, thinking that a bone might be sticking out. Finally, feeling began to return and I struggled to my feet.

What ever happened to the gentleman's course where doctors, chaplains, lawyers, and generals kind of *played* at Special Forces training? (Actually, I had taken lots of the classroom work by correspondence.) I kept telling myself that the Special Forces units needed chaplains, too. Plus, I was going to look good in that Green Beret—John Wayne, watch out!

And, by the way, where was the doctor who had talked me into this? The doc and I were roommates in jump school. He was going to be a Special Forces doctor and thought it might be a good idea for me to be one of their chaplains. He was quite a study: nonchalant to the max, aloof in a sense, but helpful to me. We became good buddies. He was dating a nurse who was in the military, overseas somewhere—Japan, I think. She became pregnant. I remember calling around for him, trying to find some way to get her out and helping him make a decision. Abortion was not in the cards. He was a hardcore Catholic. What was I thinking? I wanted to go to 'Nam. The doc thought I was crazy. He, in fact, never did go. What was I even doing in jump school? I must be crazy. How did this happen!

Being at a place like Fort Bragg and being a "leg" was like being the illegitimate son of Buffalo Bill. Being a leg—i.e., non-airborne—was like being cursed. Bragg was the only place in the world that had bumper stickers reading, "I don't brake for legs." It was not always the best mentality. Paratroopers are reported to collectively run 10 million miles a year. Just put them on Ardennes Street (the main throughfare through the 82$^\text{d}$ and always blocked off in the morning while the troops run) and they'd run to the war.

Although I was in a leg MP (military police) unit, I knew there had to be a way to get airborne. When I covered an airborne military police company, the first sergeant of the company immediately said to me, "Chaplain, there are three reasons you have to go to jump school. Number one is that you will best be able to serve my soldiers only if you are airborne. I ain't going to have no leg chaplain in my unit." The second one I'd already figured out: "If you're going to hang around Bragg and put up with all this hassle, you might as well make a little extra money."

In those days $110 extra a month was a fortune. The first sergeant continued, "The third and most important reason is that the man who started it all is from your hometown— General William C. Lee, the father of the airborne. You're probably related to him."

I knew the tiniest bit about General Lee. When I walked to school every morning as a child, I passed a historical plaque memorializing him. In later years, I would become his unofficial biographer, producing a "coffee table" book about his life.

• • •

I settled into the bus and thought again to myself, *What have I gotten myself into?* I don't think that I thought for a moment about dying or making it a year in Vietnam. I just wondered what awaited me. The fear of the unknown is probably the same with every soldier going to war. *Would I be a good chaplain? What sort of unit would I get into? What am I doing?*

*In the landscape of the soul, there is a desert,*
*a wilderness, an emptiness, and all great singers*
*must cross this desert to reach the beginning of*
*their road—Jesus, Buddha, Moses, Mohammed.*
*All wandered through the wasteland, speaking*
*to demons, speaking to empty air, listening to the*
*wind, before finding their dove, their bo tree, their*
*stone tablets, before finding their true voice. I have*
*hope for you exactly because I see you have entered*
*this desert, following in the footsteps of those few*
*who have been true teachers.*

RAY FARADAY NELSON

# Let the Fun Begin

I remember getting in shape. Running early in the morning and at night. Someone had said to me, "Get in superb shape and if you can run with the best of them, regardless of all the other stuff, it will pull you through." Great advice! When I was really hurting, I stayed with it. We were living on LeMoy street at Fort Bragg. Jackie and Meg would watch me running in the open space across from our house. *I must be crazy!* What motivated me when my lungs were about to burst was the $110 that we desperately needed.

We had just come from seminary and were very poor. Everybody we knew we seemed to owe, and the budget was stretched to the point of lots of beans and biscuits and gravy. How Jackie did it was way beyond me.

Being a military family is not easy financially; the pay is more like a stipend. The sacrifices are many. What an understatement! Over the years, as I've watched young couples, often with small children, come into the military, I've said to myself, *Do these families have a clue what they are getting into and what their lives are going to be like?* It's probably just as well they don't. Because of the peculiar nature of our culture, the country has never fully understood or appreciated the sacrifices of military families. The men are often out there doing what they love, and the families are laboring on under impossible odds.

*Vietnam divided father and son,*
*intellectual and hard hat, hawk and dove,*
*peacenik mother and John Wayne father.*
*It created a changed mood in America.*

MYRA MACPHERSON, AUTHOR OF *LONG TIME PASSING*

# C130 Whipping Down the Strip; Airborne Baby Gonna Take a Little Trip

Jump school is one of those experiences that is almost indescribable. It's a test of endurance and courage, not to mention a loss of dignity. Jumping out of a perfectly good airplane is not natural. In many ways, jump school is the "basic" for all other macho military elite training, and it does take some effort and courage to do it. I've often wondered what motivates those pursuing extreme sports or this type of military training. Those who succeed at Ranger and Seal school—and other hardcore physical training—can compete in any daring physical challenge and achievement that I know. These types of activities appeal to a niche of Americans who want to be challenged to be the best.

Jumping out of the airplane may be the easiest part. It's the preparation that's difficult, but there are reasons for all the hard work. A soldier must be in shape to meet the fitness requirements. If soldiers are winded when they get to the battle, they can't fight. It is not the ability to run twenty miles that's important—it's being physically fit enough to fight. *I didn't want to fight, just get through jump school!*

Airborne training is given in three consecutive phases: Ground Week, Tower Week, and Jump Week. My training was in August. Fort Benning, Georgia, in August has to be as close to hell on Earth as can be imagined—even the gung ho types admit it. The saying *If God wanted to give the earth an enema, He would put the hose in at Fort Benning* is right on. Buckets of sweat pour off you and the sand flies and mosquitoes are unbearable. The joke about a mosquito pulling up to a gas pump and getting thirty gallons before someone realizes it's a mosquito is not too far-fetched.

At that time, salt tabs were the order of the day. Now we don't think they did any good but then, they were thought to be essential. Thus the motto: *Two salt tablets and driving on.*

Ground Week is a week of running, marching, running, doing push-ups and other calisthenics, and learning how to do a PLF (parachute landing fall).

> *Stand up, hook up, shuffle to the door*
> *Jump right out and count to four*
> *If that chute don't open wide,*
> *I've got another one by my side.*

If I hadn't been so exhausted constantly, I would have enjoyed watching us do the PLFs. There's a system to them, and you have to do them almost seamlessly to qualify. They are graded by an instructor: balls of the feet, roll, calves of the legs, sides of the thighs, sometimes a slight brushing of the hip (this is my description, not the manual's), a little shoulder—on your feet! In practice, the feet and buttocks (the "fourth point of contact," as they're described) are the usual landing points. For the rest of one's military life, the way to say someone is stupid is, "They have their head up their fourth point of contact." Paratroopers understand.

Jumping out of the plane isn't a problem; it's the sudden stop that is. If you know how to do a proper PLF, then you can handle the sudden stop. We practiced them first from a platform three or four feet off the ground. At the end of Ground Week, we were supposed to know how to "execute with ease," as the "black hats" would say.

The "black hats" are so called because of their black baseball hats. They are the Lou Gossetts in *An Officer and a Gentleman.* They're all in fabulous shape and wear skin-tight t-shirts that make you realize they've been hanging out at the gym and waiting for their modeling job at *Men's Health* magazine. Thin waist, gigantic shoulders, and a set of lungs that would make Kate Smith envious. They are good, and they are respected.

During the training weeks, there's a certain amount of anxiety and constant harassment, and I didn't get special treatment because I was a chaplain. The fact that I was a chaplain either eluded the trainers or they had simply decided to treat me like another trainee. This was good. I got dropped for lots of push-ups—sometimes two or three hundred a day—for all kinds of offenses: not shuffling correctly, not taking up a good door position, etc.

The next step in Ground Week is jumping from a low (34-foot) tower. The tower is a mishmash of cables and winding staircases. It feels like it's 500 feet high, not 34. It evokes in some the most simple, natural fear of heights. Many a would-be paratrooper decides to call it quits there.

But I made it. After my jump from the 34-foot tower, counting to four in thousands, looking up and checking the pretend canopy, I figured I was ready for anything. This exercise requires absolute perfection, and we practiced it over and over until it was automatic.

One day I had the great privilege of being the "cable guy." During the exercise, the pulley rolls you to the end, but somebody has to be there to bring back the rope that retrieves the pulley for the next jumper. This is a grueling job, and after running several miles and doing a hundred or so push-ups at various junctures, running back and forth with that rope had me close to exhaustion. Finally, after what seemed like half the afternoon in hundred-plus degrees, one of the black hats took pity on me. *Thank you Lord!*

Tower Week is more of the same, but you go on higher towers. At 280, it's like a ride at the county fair. In fact, the original contraptions came from a world's fair in New Jersey.

Tower Week entails more running, more PLFs, jumping from the big tower that pulls you to the top and then releases you, push-ups, running—no let-up. By the time you get to Jump Week, you are so thrilled to be finishing the training that jumping out of an airplane is a piece of cake.

One jump is with just the parachute and reserve (the old T-10, which is not nearly as maneuverable as those used today, but with them you can do what is called "slip," and drive the chute around the sky). A couple of jumps are equipment jumps, where a hundred pounds or so of extra gear are added to what you're already carrying. You're hardly able to move. You have to go to the bathroom—in both ways. Misery knows no bounds. Usually there's a night jump. The joke is that for many, all jumps are night jumps—they jump with their eyes closed.

Finally you graduate, and those silver wings are pinned upon your chest. Surprisingly, very few people die from leaping out of airplanes—maybe two a year—a miniscule number compared to how many jump, which is reported to be 110,000 or so a year. Of course, if you are one of the two, it is a hundred percent.

> *Those silver wings upon my chest*
> *I am one of America's best.*

## The Father of the Airborne

General William C. Lee is the father of the American airborne. Among America's World War II heroes, he was without peer in bringing paratroopers into modern warfare, yet few besides those who know the history of the Airborne are aware of his enormous achievements.

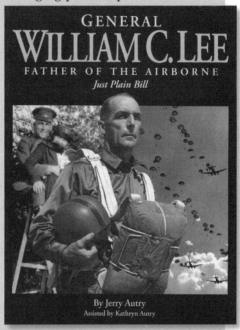

GENERAL
# WILLIAM C. LEE
FATHER OF THE AIRBORNE
*Just Plain Bill*

By Jerry Autry
Assisted by Kathryn Autry

While serving on special duty as an officer in a French tank unit, he saw German paratroopers firsthand and began to promote the idea as a tactical necessity in the American military. To him, a force that would parachute behind enemy lines made sense. For a long time, his voice cried in the wilderness, but then fate intervened.

President and Mrs. Roosevelt were at their home in Hyde Park, New York, and while watching a newsreel, saw a segment having to do with German paratroopers. The President turned to his military aide and said, "Do we have anything like that in our army?" The aide didn't know but vowed to find out. His search led him to the only person in the entire military who was a proponent of an airborne force, an obscure major named Bill Lee.

With an indomitable will and against almost impossible odds, Bill Lee brought the American paratrooper into reality.

*Indeed we are running away all the time*
*to avoid coming face to face*
*with our real selves.*

ANONYMOUS

# If I Die on an Old Drop Zone, Box Me Up and Ship Me Home

The airborne has many traditions—things like prop blasts, initiations, various degrees of torture—but all in all, tradition is what being a paratrooper is all about. The paratrooper often chafes when described as a "parachutist." Anybody can be a *parachutist*, but being a *paratrooper* takes soul. It's the willingness to scale any mountain, ford any river, or leap tall buildings at a single bound. It's the heart! The fraternity of the airborne is reinforced over and over throughout one's military career. A friend said it like this: *Paratroopers have an all-purpose affirmation for one another—a greeting, a farewell, an amen.* When they say, "Airborne," they are declaring membership in an elite group meticulously trained to conquer danger. *Airborne* isn't just a motto or a standard, it is a passion.

Paratroopers love to tell "jump" stories. When I was the Division Chaplain in the 82ᵈ Airborne Division, one of the biggest problems I had with my chaplains was keeping them from telling jump stories in the pulpit. I'd say, "Come on guys, this is an airborne division. Everyone in this Division is a paratrooper and their families have already heard all their stories." I finally had to give up.

Even though I was a trainee in jump school and essentially was having the same training as everybody else, to the troops I was still a chaplain, and when they got a chance, they came to see me. It was girlfriend problems, wife and family issues, getting out of the Army, not wanting to go to Vietnam. You name it.

Jump school was harassment—or better said, it was "in your face." This was part of the plan and it was designed to test trainees' ability to keep cool and convince them of the elite nature of the airborne. I remember one lieutenant whose face is indelibly etched in my brain. He was a blast, especially at leading cadence. I don't know where he got all the stuff. This was his favorite, and we sang it a thousand times:

> *I want to be an airborne ranger,*
> *I want to live a life of danger,*
> *I want to go to Vietnam,*
> *I want to kill some Vietcong.*
> *Airborne, Airborne.*

His bravado masked an underlying fear of heights, and he confessed to me that the thought of jumping out of an airplane was unfathomable. He was scared big-time. The closer we got to going out of that plane door, the more sedate and the more attached to me he became. I kept trying to reassure him.

The day of the first jump, here we were, all assembled in full parachute regalia: chute, reserve chute, checked out, miserable, scared, apprehensive. Let's get it on! "OK, men, today you are going to be airborne. Forty-eighth company has done its job. We gave you a week on the ground teaching you how to properly exit an aircraft. Then we had some fun by letting you jump out of a little tower and then fall from a nice high tower. Now, you sorry legs, it's showtime." A black hat sergeant bellowed this speech like he'd made it before.

The lieutenant edged over to me. "Chaplain, I'm sicker'n hell," he said.

"You'll be all right when that wind hits you in the face," I replied.

"Chaplain, I can't do it."

"Sure, you can." I tried to sound more confident than I felt.

I wasn't even sure *I* could do it. There's always a nagging doubt about leaping into thin air. Then something kicks in. You'll do it if you know you're going to die. Jumping is preferable to dying. At least that's what I was telling myself.

"You know you'll go out that door even if you're puking all the way," I said, patting him on the back. He was a West Point graduate, and I knew he'd been through worse.

"I can't do it. What if my chute don't open or I get a Mae West?" (A "Mae West" is when a paratrooper's static lines, those leading to his chute, get wrapped around the chute itself. This can cause a kind of brassiere look, hence Mae West. Instead of one big billowing chute that somewhat gently takes you downward, there are two smaller chutes, which can cause a much faster rate of drop. This is dangerous; it could cause injury or death. During jump school, troopers learn to exit the aircraft vigorously, because a Mae West is more likely to happen when a paratrooper simply falls out the door).

"Ah, come on, lieutenant. Those things don't really happen, they just been BS-ing us."

"I can't do it. I'm going to tell the jumpmaster I want out."

I reached out and grabbed him: "Come on—everybody gets shook. I've never jumped out of a plane either. We'll do it together." *What am I doing? I must be crazy. I am crazy.*

For a moment, he seemed to accept it and then, "No, I can't, Chaplain, I'm sorry. I know what's going to happen to me. I'm going to buy the farm."

"No, you're not. I'm in the same stick. We'll go out together." *Why am I doing this; I need to be worrying about myself.*

For what seemed like forever, we stood, hunched over, both having to go to the bathroom. We started moving across the runway to the plane. What a sorry sight we must have been. The lieutenant kept trying to get out of line and I kept nudging him along. Finally, I edged myself around to the side and pushed him along. As I think of it now, I didn't know what I was doing. It was all I could do to keep *myself* together. This was definitely no time to be my brother's keeper. But somehow, I was there. I guess the chaplain gene kicked in. The reluctant paratrooper made a move to speak to the jumpmaster, but I pushed him up the steps into the plane before he could speak. *What am I doing?* We sat down on the webbed straps lashed along the side of the plane, and we were a silent group as the C130 workhorse roared down the runway and into the air.

We were packed in like sardines, not like the good days to come when jumping from C141 jets would be pretty comfortable. The C47s and C130s were designed for misery, and we *were* miserable. I glanced at the jumpmaster a time or two, and our eyes seemed to hold for a second. It could have been my imagination, but later on, when *I* became a jumpmaster, I knew the drill—there's always some trooper who doesn't want to jump and at the last minute decides to opt out.

Whether to let him is a heavy decision for the jump-master. If he lets him out of the jump, the young trooper will have to live with it all of his life. In the macho and unforgiving 82$^\text{d}$, if a soldier refuses to jump, the rule is that before the sun sets, he is out of the division. Disgraced! If the jumpmaster *does* get the soldier out the door and something bad happens, the jumpmaster's own career may be ruined. There's also the matter of getting the scared trooper out the door without jeopardizing the other paratroopers. It's no easy task, and the decision must be made in a split second. All of us who have been in the jumpmaster's shoes know how difficult it is. Almost 100 percent of the time, if the trooper gets out the door on his first jump, he's OK. Here I was helping out the jumpmaster and didn't know which end was up myself.

Twenty minutes later, the jumpmaster stood with his mouth moving. Although we heard nothing, everyone knew exactly what he was saying. My lieutenant had his head in his hands. "Outboard personnel stand up, check equipment, sound off for equipment check, stand in the door." The shuffle started—people moved toward the door. In a second, the green light flashed. My trooper folded up in front of me like a wet noodle. I don't know what possessed me, but I reached down and wedged him between myself and the next GI's equipment and pushed him along toward the door.

At the door, the jumpmaster was shouting, "Stand in the door," and as each guy moved into the doorway, he patted him on the rump. "Go." After the first one or two, they just flew out of the door, and the plane was emptied, it seemed, in milliseconds.

When my guy didn't move like the rest, the jumpmaster looked up. I muscled the lieutenant into the doorway, pushed him out, and went out almost on top of him. When my chute opened, I was very grateful to feel the thud and to look up and see that billowing canopy. *Thank you, Lord!*

I scanned the skies looking for the lieutenant, but didn't see him. Because of the wind, I knew he could be 25 to 50 yards from me. I had a great ride down. The quiet of it was mixed with gratitude—all the training had worked! When I hit the ground, not a perfect PLF but acceptable, there was still no sign of my lieutenant. He could be dead. He could have passed out when he hit the wind and fallen like a lifeless dummy. He could have broken all his bones when he hit the ground, and it would all be my fault. *Why did I have to interfere? Nobody appointed me God.* I was sick to my stomach.

After gathering up our chutes and stuffing them into our kit bags, we had to jog about half a mile to an assembly point. When I got there, beside the truck were several troopers jostling and boasting about their jumps, and above all the voices could be heard the lieutenant—"Man, I hit that door and popped right out to a Mae West. I shook it out with no sweat and did a perfect PLF!" He glanced up at me and grinned.

*In the 82ᵈ, just line us up on Ardennes and
we'll run to the war. If there is a hard way
to do it and give us more pain, bring it on!*

A PFC IN HQ. CO, 82D AIRBORNE DIVISION

# Cherries and
# Bring on the Suffering

We went inside a gate—guarded by a couple of MPs—
who stopped us briefly, took one look inside the bus,
smiled, and motioned us in. I didn't realize it then, but I
should have known the smile was a smirk—*cherries, a year
in this hellhole.* The sign read, "Welcome to 90ᵗʰ Replacement
Battalion." It was apparent already that the United States
was a presence in Vietnam. The little amenities were
everywhere. We rode through a small built-up section that
could easily have been mistaken for one of those cowboy-
western towns; the only things missing were the hitching
rails. It was all plywood.

An NCO (noncommissioned officer) who had boarded
at the first stop delivered our first speech: "Men, welcome

to the Republic of South Vietnam. It's going to be a year of FTA. Now, I know you think you know what it means, but I can't say it because of the chaplain. It really means 'fun, travel, and adventure.'" He glanced at me, smiled, and went on. "Many of you may think you're ready to face the enemy, but everything over here is measured on the return trip. Make sure you're on it."

He looked down as if in deep thought and then continued: "When you are sitting out on patrol or in the jungle and hear the distant knocking of bamboo on bamboo—the equivalent of the American Indian smoke signals—you can just know 'Sir Charles' is out there. Respect him before you kill him, and you'll make this return ride. I'll be waiting for you." I thought it was pretty poignant.

We piled off the bus and a somewhat pudgy sergeant took over. He said, "Enlisted here and officers here." The old timers knew exactly what to do. "Men, you are now in Vietnam. Tomorrow, you'll be getting your unit assignments, but while you're here, you're my responsibility. You men may not think so, but we are at war, and you can get your ass killed right here in Long Binh just as easy as when you are in the field." He paused. "Hell, everywhere over in this godforsaken place is the field, and don't forget it. I don't want none of you to get more than 25 yards from this building. The chow hall is in building 1054. Go and be back for formation at 1745. Fall out."

Chow was served at 1700. I was still calculating how to make seventeen hundred into five o'clock. It was hot and sticky. "Don't forget your salt tabs," the fat sergeant said, as though reading my mind on the hot and sticky. The long building where we were to bunk was just that—long and devoid of pictures from home. I sat on the bunk to write a letter to Jackie and Meg. I had decided to write every day regardless of the circumstances. I did.

*Dear* (I'll leave out the mushy stuff), *Well, here I am, finally made it. Not any real way to describe it, hot and hot, think tobacco fields of NC. Hope you are doing OK.* I said more and I tried to picture where they were and what they were doing. They were with Jackie's folks—a nice thing for the folks to do, and I've always been appreciative. Just recently, Jackie was telling me that every day for a whole year, her dad took Meg downtown to the drugstore and bought her ice cream. The soda shop was on the square in Laurens, South Carolina, and was right out of a 1940s film—think the movie *Majestic*.

That night at the 90th Replacement did not pass easily or quickly. I was a chaplain and acted like one, talking to the men, supplying a little "showtime." Talking was in my nature, and the guys were happy to chat—we talked and talked, and before I knew it, morning had arrived. Few men had anything to say about their apprehensions, including me.

The sounds of Vietnam were many—in the distance, gunfire of some sort, with flares lighting up the sky. Artillery howitzers blazing away. Rain on the roof. A bunch of GIs laughing and talking at the other end of the building.

I knew that a few of the enlisted guys had gotten tabbed to pull guard duty. Most of the new guys didn't even have weapons. I thought, this is great, we are all green as grass, don't have a clue as to what to expect, and we're out here pulling guard duty. *Welcome to the Nam!*

• • •

I could not be content just to be a chaplain, so after jump school I decided to take the Special Forces course. "Prefix 3" it was called. I wanted to go to war with the best. My way of thinking then was that the Green Berets were the best. I was caught up in the mystique of it all and had come to admire the Special Forces chaplains. I actually got to know only one really well. He helped in Vacation Bible School (VBS). How tough is that?

That this chaplain taught VBS was always a little humorous to me, but VBS was also something that made being a chaplain very real. The VBS this chaplain helped with was for the children and families on military posts. If they had been out in the civilian world and attending church, they would have been going to Vacation Bible School, so why not have it in the military? In a sense, having it is justification for the chaplaincy. After all, this chaplain was into being a pastor and having VBS long before he was a soldier.

When a group challenged the constitutionality of the chaplaincy, the Supreme Court decided that a soldier should have the same things available to him and his family in the military as he did as a civilian. He did not give up his birthright as a citizen when he became a soldier.

But the irony of holding VBS on a military post was not lost on me. It seemed a little incongruent—as if something was not quite right. Here we were, at least some of us, these macho chaplains caught up in the military world— gung ho, kill, kill, kill—and now we were doing VBS! Got to love it. Let's face it—being a chaplain in the military was a little on the weird side anyhow. I never got over thinking that, but for me, it fit.

• • •

Americans were present and accounted for in Vietnam. Soon there would be gyms, bars, hot tubs and saunas, volleyball nets—all the sorts of things that Americans bring in to remind them of the good old USA. This Americanizing of war (not the weapons and tactics) creeps up on you, making war more palatable, which we don't want to do.

*"Sometimes I'm scared and I miss my
children but we're doing the best we can
and we know the American people support
us. I can't imagine what it must have been
like for Vietnam veterans to come home
and not be supported."*

AN AIR FORCE SERGEANT IN IRAQ, VETERANS DAY, 2003

# I Want to Move Right into Breaking Bricks

(Reference to all the time spent warming up when involved
in Tae Kwon Do, a Korean martial art.)

The beginning of my interest in the chaplaincy is hard to pinpoint. My family has always been military. All four of my brothers were in the military. My brother Raz was a Marine on Guadalcanal. Corbett was in twice. Once was at the end of World War II, but he was discovered to be too young and was unceremoniously let go, to hear him tell it. Later on, he went in again and went overseas during peacetime to Italy. Still, to this day, he talks about it and wonders, "What if?" Charles was in Korea as an artillery forward observer with the 1st Cavalry and was wounded badly. His life was quite a saga. I was older when he was in the service and able to grasp what was happening more than I had been when Raz and Corb were fighting their wars. My mother went often to the mailbox to see if there was mail from Chuck, who, as I remember, was not long on correspondence.

The day that Ms. McSwain, a venerable Red Cross worker, came to our house to inform my parents that Chuck had been wounded is one I'll always remember. I was 12 years old. No one knew the severity of his injuries, but suddenly visions of Audie Murphy coming up the drive with one leg, hoping he would still be accepted by the family, jumped all over my consciousness. My mom was always a little into high drama.

The event I remember most clearly was when Charles was to come home on leave from Fort Sill. Apparently his best friend was a black GI and he wanted to bring him to visit. When he was told it "might not be a good idea," he went into orbit.

"If he can't come, neither will I!"

This was my first look at racism, and what a difference the exposure of the military made. Chuck was forever a champion of the downtrodden. Later on—thirty years plus down the road as a small town councilman—he was still fighting the battles for the downtrodden and the "black man," as he described the race.

The brother next to me in age, Wallace, was in the Navy. Hop, we called him. We jokingly said we weren't sure that our mom didn't have an affair, as Wallace didn't seem like the rest of us—he's quiet—an introvert. He seemed like he was 40 when he was born.

Looking back, I realize that my interest in the military began at an early age, when I became aware of my brothers' military portraits on our fireplace mantel. Mom was very proud of that mantel display. They were in dress uniform from oldest to youngest: Raz, Navy; Corb, Army; Charles, Army; Wallace, Navy. I was the only one missing. When the ministry became my calling, thoughts of those portraits lingered as if someone had tattooed them on my forehead. *How could I ever be on that mantel now? What a sacrifice I was making!*

Figuring it all out—and eventually wearing the uniform—seems humorous now. As a youngster, I remember the soldiers from Fort Bragg strutting around in their jump boots stealing all the girls, or so I thought. Maybe that had an influence on what I wanted to do.

I was in my own world at seminary, newly married, and trying to look to the future. But the sense of impending events as the Vietnam situation heated up heavily influenced the direction I'd follow. After all, serving was what the ministry was about—and where better to serve than at war.

*"Some people are strengthened by failure, and others are defeated by it. Who survives and who does not has little to do with money or advantage; it depends more on inner strength of character—a primitive toughness that protects the self and will not let mere external events destroy it."*

FROM THE BOOK *WHEN SMART PEOPLE FAIL,*
BY CAROLE HYATT AND LINDA GOTTLIEB

# You're in the Army now, You're not Behind a Plow

My first duty assigment after seminary was Fort Bragg, North Carolina. To me, Fort Bragg was the only place in the world. Californians have a Fort Bragg too, but the one in North Carolina is the place to be—Home of the Airborne, mainly the 82$^{nd}$ Airborne Division. Driving onto Bragg was like riding into a new world of wonderment.

Over the years, this post has seen just about every aspect of the military. In a sense, it represents an alien environment about which very few in the public have a clue. The military has always been a type of subculture with its own laws, society, protocols, and traditions. When I hear old soldiers talk or see old movies like *From Here to Eternity*, I understand that this is an element of society that is unto itself. And it's one that has existed as long as we've had a military.

Chaplains in the Army are assigned to units, and this sets them apart from chaplains in other services. In the Air Force and Navy, chaplains are assigned to a base or ship. Marine chaplains are actually Navy chaplains temporarily assigned to Marine units.

My initial assignment was to a military police unit. I'm not going to name units or names to protect the innocent and avoid disparaging anyone's name or reputation. What I remember about that unit could fill two books. It was a great one to have as a first assignment. I had some clashes with young commanders, but most were happy to have me.

Being a soldier advocate and troubleshooter was how I interpreted my job. I didn't come to this view by myself. My boss's constant reinforcement included: "Anything that has to do with the morale of the troops is your business." I never forgot his words, and they set the stage for how I interpreted my entire military ministry. As I was to learn throughout my not-so-illustrious military career, the commander and how he gives you power was the key.

The military police provided a functional challenge, and learning my way around their nuances and military jargon was no small thing, but I had to do it, because part of my duties included being the stockade (jail) chaplain.

Talk about an experience! I had worked in jail ministry during my college days when I was in the Ministerial Union. One of our duties was to preach every Friday night at the county jail to a "captive" audience. As we went from cell to cell, it became apparent that those who were listening wanted us to do something—to mail a letter, give them spare change, whatever. And unfortunately, sometimes the chaplain or preacher was the one to con.

These were the days of the draft, and most of those in military jails had been AWOL (absent without leave). There were other crimes, but mainly they had to do with the small stuff. Often soldiers who went to jail would never have been subject to incarceration if they hadn't been in the military—on the outside, there is no AWOL.

What makes the military is people, and in this case, there was plenty of personality to go around. The XO (executive officer), who really ran the unit, was a great guy. Let's call him Will. At five feet five, he had a little bit of a Napoleonic complex, but he was a great guy. Will was nobody's fool, tough as nails, and could cut you off at the knees before you could blink an eye.

In our unit, we had a detachment of warrant officers—a bunch of older CID (criminal investigators division) types: think John Travolta in *The General's Daughter*. I got to know these guys pretty well—especially the enlisted guys who did the scut work: background checks, investigating petty crime, etc. But according to Will, the CID could screw up a two-car funeral procession. They could take a tiny crime and make it into a gigantic criminal case with lots of speculative evidence. Before their investigation ended, there *would* be a crime.

I think Will respected these guys, but from time to time, he had to let them know who was in charge. Usually, the commander of their detachment was a young lieutenant who knew nothing. More than likely, he was brand-new to the Army and didn't know his posterior from a hole in the ground. Will was the ever-present mentor to all of us green-as-grass, newly minted Army officers.

For instance, chaplains were trained in theology and counseling, but we needed guidance on how best to fit into the unit if we outranked others. Will was our mentor. Something he did regularly made quite an impression on me. He would call the warrant officers to a meeting and chitchat for a moment or two. Then he'd go to the blackboard and, starting way down at the bottom, he'd write, WO 1 (warrant officer). And, then above it, he would write WO 2 and continue on—WO 3, WO 4—and then in big letters at the top, 01, which is the number designation for a second lieutenant. His point was clear. The warrant officers were seasoned. They knew their stuff, but the lieutenant was the ranking officer and he was in charge. Will would not tolerate them being disrespectful to a young officer regardless of how unseasoned—and, on occasion, incompetent—he might be.

Will expected no insubordination from the warrant officers, and they understood this. Their commander, a lieutenant, was extremely naïve. He was an infantry officer who had been commissioned through ROTC and detailed to the military police for a year. He was reading *War and Peace,* and to keep track of the characters he had his entire office plastered with poster board outlining the plots and players; he claimed it helped him in his job. What was funny about him was that he knew he was just filling space. He kept saying he was saving himself for the big push, which in those days was Vietnam. He left the unit to go to Vietnam after I had been there a couple of months and was killed in December 1968.

My experiences at Bragg were legion. It was 1967; Vietnam was heating up; casualties were mounting; and I was assigned to a notification team—as were all the chaplains—to inform families that their sons had been killed in the line of duty in Vietnam, fighting for their country.

Fayetteville, the home of Fort Bragg, is probably the most patriotic city in America, and the people are proud of their history. Fayetteville has a wonderful modern museum honoring the history of the military. Fort Bragg itself is the Home of the Airborne, Special Forces (Green Berets), and at least two or three other museums.

Fort Bragg is not unlike a college campus. When soldiers are not on duty, they can be seen in high school letter jackets, looking like a bunch of kids just coming from class. At night, it reminds me of fraternity row on my old college campus. Domino's Pizza trucks pull in at any hour—two in the morning or later is more the rule than the exception. The post a beehive of activity—America's young men and women ready to go to war at the drop of a hat. I was proud to be part of this.

One day I was given an assignment to perform the funeral for a sergeant first class who had been killed in Vietnam. We had a firing squad of six members and an honor guard of another six, plus a staff sergeant who was in charge. We were going to Camden, South Carolina, for the funeral, and we traveled in an Army vehicle and two vans. We made the sixty or so miles to Camden and had the funeral—the family was very sad but somewhat stoic as I remember. They were a military family steeped in tradition. From what I could tell, they had always lived with the idea that this career NCO could forfeit his life in war.

When we departed, it was 6:00 PM, nearly time for dinner (supper, it's called in the South). I suggested that once we got out of town, we should find a place for chow. The sergeant of the guard was hesitant, but I said, "Let's do it." We stopped at a nice truck stop on the edge of town. We walked in, and suddenly it seemed as quiet as death.

We were proud soldiers, dressed to the nines: bloused boots, badges and patches, and looking good. As I sat down, a waitress came up to me and said, rather loudly and forcefully, "We don't serve niggers."

Up until that time, I had not even thought of anything relating to race. We had in our group blacks, Hispanics, and at least one Native American. Most of us were white guys. This was America! It simply never dawned on me that here it was 1967; the Supreme Court decision integrating the schools had happened in 1954. Martin Luther King made his famous speech in 1963, and the civil rights bill had been passed the year before we arrived at the truck stop. Here were American soldiers doing their duty who were not even allowed to eat because of the color of their skin. This single event changed my life forever in terms of how I saw race relations and the actions I took to counter racism whenever I faced it.

• • •

Vietnam loomed heavily upon us all, and for the military, it was our purpose. What the civilian community never really understands is that by and large, soldiers are trained to go to war, and that is what they want to do—they look forward to it, especially in the initial stages. War gets old, like it did in Vietnam—like it's doing in Iraq. But basically, going to war is what the military exists to do. I was constantly worried that Vietnam would be over with before I made it there.

Most of my battalion (700–1000 people) had not been to Vietnam yet. We had one lieutenant who was just back. He loved to tell war stories and was proud to have the war behind him. The BS factor was big-time with him. He had been with the unit that most of my battalion would join, the 716 MP Company, which dealt with security of Saigon and the American Embassy. The 716 MP guarding the American Embassy in Vietnam became somewhat infamous when the news media reported that the VC (Vietcong) had taken over the embassy, which was not true. In fact, the issue became a celebrated cause. In later years, as the Vietnam war was debated, the reporter who wrote the story of the embassy takeover was discovered to have lied—he hadn't even been in the area.

*I believe God knows what he's doing.*
*I'm not worried."*

A YOUNG SOLDIER ON HIS WAY TO IRAQ

# Shoot to Kill, Shoot to Kill

Lieutenant O, as we called him, was a lot of fun. He saw himself as the battalion playboy and lived in a bachelor pad off Fort Bragg, which quickly became infamous for parties. He got reined in, however, when he and the wife of one of the other lieutenants got a little too friendly. I often wondered what people thought would happen. You put a bunch of young people in an environment like a swanky bachelor pad and add alcohol—things will happen or come close to happening. Parties, alcohol, and young people occur in civilian life, but in the military, there's a sense of nonpermanence—these young officers didn't expect to be around tomorrow. They'd either be out of the Army, reassigned, or off to Vietnam, so their motto was, *Don't waste time—get to know each other.* Most didn't even think about the potential for emotional disaster.

This concept was not unique to them. The colonel was quite a character study. Good commander, but stiff as a board. He tried to be one of the boys but couldn't manage it. In those days, before alcohol became uncool and at times illegal, happy hour and battalion social hours were a must. The good colonel tried, but he could dampen the liveliest gathering. I always got a kick out of him—more after I left the battalion than when I was in it. I will have to say, however, that when called to lead, he stood tall. Those were the days of riots, and our unit was trained for riot control.

We went to Washington for the infamous March on the Pentagon, and the colonel took control. Once when I wanted to have a service, he nixed it. "No way are we having the troops spread out all over this maze." I was disappointed, but that was good leadership—he took charge!

What always amazed me about him was how good his uniform looked on him. The rest of us, after being up all night, hanging out in some tunnel in Washington with the carbon monoxide eating away at us, looked like death warmed over. Not him; he looked like he just stepped out of a bandbox, neatly pressed, standing tall. I was always blown away.

He was one of these uncomfortable men—a high introvert who had to work hard to project even a semblance of friendliness or civility. He even had a little touch of the commander in *The Mutiny on the Bounty* with his steel balls. I was in his office once, standing before his desk with some other people. He went on and on about an issue; it seems like he talked for hours. I must have leaned over and rested my hand on his desk. After he finished his talk, he asked everybody to leave but me and then went into an elaborate statement and topped it off with, "Please don't put your hand on my desk."

• • •

These were the sixties, and the Vietnam War had heated up. Here we were in Washington in '68 with the March on Washington and rioting. We camped out in the Pentagon. The crowning event, I remember, was one night looking for a place to sleep. We went into a big, fabulous-looking room with a carpet that was appealing to use as a mattress. We sacked out, and the next morning, when I woke up, I found myself lying under a huge conference table. Gigantic globs of gum were stuck all over the underside of this beautiful mahogany table. Someone later told me that it was the conference room for the Secretary of Defense and the Joint Chiefs of Staff. No wonder we were in a quagmire in Vietnam. Our leaders were chewing their gum and stowing it under a table!

Our first trip to Washington—for the March on the Pentagon—had a little party atmosphere to it. The military policemen were around 18 years old, and it's not like they grew up on an alien planet. Many of the marchers were about the same age. They were holding the line—the mythical one drawn in the sand. The MPs were standing just a few feet from the marchers. Who knows what difference there was in their ideologies, but they were young. Some marchers put flowers in the barrels of the soldiers' weapons. Some of the soldiers probably wished they were on the other side. A few, in some clandestine way, exchanged phone numbers. Later on someone told me that at least two marriages came from that experience. I wouldn't doubt it.

Martin Luther King's assassination brought us back to Washington a second time. Rioting was widespread, there was a curfew, and the whole thing was bizarre—a little like one of those Bruce Willis *Die Hard* movies. Fires were burning. We were there, but somehow it seemed unreal. My most memorable event amid the chaos was funny. The military police were driving their jeeps with civilian police officers as passengers. One night, I hitched a ride, and we came to a stop light with about 15 minutes to go before curfew. The idea was that with a curfew, all the folks would be off the streets, the trouble would stop and the night would be peaceful. Anybody still out after curfew must be up to mischief.

We stopped at a light, and here came a very old woman. She started across the street in front of us. She looked us over, looked to her right and then to her left, cupped her hands around her mouth and whispered to us, "Shoot to kill, shoot to kill." We busted out laughing.

• • •

I left the unit with some fanfare, driving out while the guys were still camped out over by the Park Service headquarters. The XO had arranged for the troops to line the road as we drove out on the way to the airport.

One thing I learned early on about the military is that it is a fraternity in a sense. We're set apart by the fact that we wear a uniform, but it's much more than that.

Somehow, we all know the rules. We understand them, and we're all in it together. It is hard not to understand that the fraternity is, in varying degrees, special. The troops gripe, they feel put-upon, but for the most part, they feel they're doing something. I've met few folks who, if we discussed it, didn't seem to feel that they'd missed something by not serving. They had chosen not to have this sort of rite of passage.

• • •

Getting ready to go off to war is one tough proposition. There really is no easy way to do it. No way to prepare. You get what the military calls a "leave." Vacation. You're happy to have this time, this respite, but there's an ever-present cloud hanging over your head—fear of the unknown—what to expect? How is it going to be? Are you brave enough? If you get into combat, can you measure up?

There is the pain of leaving your family—the enormous pain! In my case, Meg was five, and she knew something was going on but not quite what it was. I will never forget sitting on the plane at the Spartanburg, South Carolina, airport on my way to Vietnam by way of Travis. The pain, literally physical, was the most intense I can ever remember. I could see the faint outline in the window of Jackie and Meg watching. Going through the door to the plane was excruciating. Meg was sobbing uncontrollably and holding onto my leg. She would not let go and would not be comforted. I didn't want to cry; after all, I was a paratrooper.

The plane sat on the runway for what seemed to be an eternity. It wasn't only the leaving that was difficult; it was the apprehension—the gamut of emotions. Going to Vietnam, I knew in my heart, was the right thing to do and what I wanted to do. I was a soldier and it was what was happening, but even with all of those feelings, still, it was very, very painful. Vietnam was defining for me, and, in a sense, it was also our country's pivotal time, and I wanted to participate in it.

I did and I'm glad.

*Stand up, hook up,*
*Shuffle to the door,*
*Jump right out and count to four.*
*If that chute don't open wide,*
*I've got another one by my side.*

AIRBORNE CHANT

# Can't Wait to Get to Vietnam

The flight to San Francisco was fairly uneventful other than that the tightness in my chest would not go away. It has to be the hardest thing I've ever done. I don't think civilians can know how many sacrifices military families make. I could write a book about Jackie and Meg's year with her folks and how we tried to stay connected. The pivotal event in my life was in front of me and I was getting to it. I felt a little better when we landed. It was a combination of excitement and apprehension. I had never been out West before and to me, San Francisco was a mythical place on the Left Coast. I didn't identify with it then, and riding through it seeing the downtown, I had no earthly idea about Haight/Ashbury or the year of love or the "crazies" (aka normal San Franciscans). Even in those days, the bizarre in San Francisco was thought to be normal. I was just passing through.

Travis Air Force Base was the departure point for the Nam and the ride up on the bus was memorable. Things looked pretty drab, none of the greenery that was so familiar in North Carolina. The liaison officer who met us at SFO seemed jaded. He had on greens and lots of medals and badges. He was a sergeant first class, I think. I was still in a bit of a daze. Like everyone else, I had a big flight bag and a duffel bag. About 25 of us had been waiting for a while. Vietnam was building up and hordes of GIs on the way to Nam were a three-or-four-times-a-day occurrence.

We went through an entrance gate at Travis, a busy place—Air Force types were everywhere. We wound around several streets and buildings and ended up at a processing point. We got processed in and assigned a room and were told we'd be on our way to Vietnam in a day or two—more info would be forthcoming. For some weird reason, I was incredibly patient, and patience isn't one of my strong points. After I put my gear down, I wrote a letter to Jackie, the first one of many to follow. (I wish I had it now—what did I say?)

The tightness in my chest and the literal pain of departure dissipated a little, and I became excited about the upcoming adventure. I walked out to find a mailbox and immediately encountered a Signal guy (Signal is the communications branch of the Army).

How did I know he was a Signal guy? I always look at a person's branch. Will, in my MP unit, had crazy ideas about the sort of people who end up in particular branches. The infantry are adventurers and crazy. (He didn't mention that they were cannon fodder in Nam.) Mention MPs and he'd say, "They're the intelligent types; want to do something useful and love guns." There'd always be a guffaw after that.

"Now, the ones you want to stay away from?" he'd say. "The Signal guys—they're guys who should still be walking around wearing a pocket protector," meaning they should have remained civilians.

Anyhow, this Signal guy asked, "Chaplain, want to go to Frisco with a few of us?"

"I don't think so," I answered.

"Hey, how about Valley Jo then?" *Valley Jo.* Even to my country bumpkin ears, Valley Jo didn't sound like the name of a city. But he persisted in calling it that, so I followed his lead. Later I mentioned it to someone else who laughed and corrected my pronunciation of *Vallejo* (va-lay'-ho). I said, "Well, I've just started wearing shoes, you know." To this day I laugh about it.

We caught a bus into Vallejo and walked around, and the next thing I knew we were heading to San Francisco. I kept rationalizing that it would help me get my mind off the pain of separation. *Here I was being led around by a Signal officer. Give me a break!*

In Nam, I'd get to know another Signal guy well. The Signal types were forever the whipping boys of everybody, or so it seemed. Everything got blamed on them. Things were not often their fault, but communication is important in war and the saying, "If you ain't got commo, you ain't got shit" is about as right-on as it is crude. If I had been a little more savvy, I would definitely have been better off staying at Travis.

We got to San Francisco and immediately ended up in North Beach. I think the taxi driver took one look, sized us up, and decided that North Beach and the risqué section of San Francisco was our lot. There were huge marquees with pictures of Carol Doda, the queen of strippers. Guys we met on the street and my Signal buddy were constantly trying to get me into strip joints. Somehow it reminded me of the county fair. Talk about naïve. I was absolutely overwhelmed, and a Vietnam firefight would have seemed a welcome relief.

Finally, my Signal bud led us into a joint that looked relatively tame. We sat at the bar and the bartender came over and said, "Could I see your identification?" I didn't think much about it at the time, but why did he want to see our IDs? I could hardly believe we looked underage. I immediately gave him my green active duty military ID because I was proud of being a soldier. Almost as if rehearsed, he turned it over and looked at the back of it. In those days, the chaplain's ID card had a distinctive cross, indicating that he was a noncombatant per the Geneva Convention. The bartender looked at me and said, "You a 'Father?'"

I didn't know if he meant, "Do you have children" or "Are you a priest?" As I was trying to stammer out the fact I was a Protestant—or to go to the bathroom in my pants—this guy says to the whole bar, "Hey, this guy is a priest and he's on his way to Vietnam." Every head in the place turned and all of sudden, people were coming over, shaking my hand, and three drinks suddenly appeared in front of me.

I didn't know what to do, but finally managed to say something and walked out the door. I'm sure they felt I was ungrateful, but just getting out of there was my goal. I had no clue that this would possibly be the last gesture of appreciation for Vietnam vets that anyone in San Francisco would make.

I wish I could say that this was the end of my San Francisco adventure, but I was not that lucky. Mr. Signal reappeared, and I said, "I want to get back to Travis." Before I knew it, we had moved out of the North Beach area, and he said, "Here's a nice place; they've probably got a piano bar." Well, it looked pretty tame: no dancing, strippers, or anybody wanting to see our IDs. I ordered a Coke and gave the waitress a twenty. I didn't have many of them. She sized me up, I guess, as she disappeared, and never did return with my change. No respect for America's warriors! I don't know how we finally got out of there and back to Travis, but I didn't leave the base again until three days later, when we boarded the Big Iron Bird for Vietnam.

*If I were hanged on the highest hill,*
*I know whose love would follow me still,*
*Mother o' mine, O mother o' mine!*
*If I were drowned in the deepest sea,*
*I know whose tears would come down to me,*
*Mother o' mine, O mother o' mine!*
*If I were damned o' body and soul,*
*I know whose prayers would make me whole,*
*Mother o' mine, O mother o' mine!*

RUDYARD KIPLING

# Addled by the Army

(or How I Become a Military Chaplain)

My mom would say you were "addled" if you put your head inside a bell and then had someone ring it. Get the picture? Someone who's addled is confused; can't figure it out; doesn't know which end is up. I've got a manuscript floating around somewhere about my experiences at my wonderful little church before I went into the Army. At first I called it, *A Slice of Pie*, then I went to using a phrase from Grantland Rice's poem, *Don't Hurry, Don't Worry and Don't Forget to Smell the Flowers*. Then I even went back to the original name of the community, *Triangle*. You might say that the title was better than the book.

I loved my little church. Although it was a student pastorate, it was important to me. However, my ADD (attention deficit disorder) was in high gear.

Every pastor—I think this was how it worked—got a letter saying how badly chaplains were needed in the military. I took the letter personally. Vietnam was heating up and there were only a thousand or so chaplains in the military; they needed at least five thousand. I didn't have a clue about what it would be like, but it all sounded good and was an answer to a prayer.

The truth, in many ways, was that I would have done anything to escape my little church. Not that it was bad. In most ways, it was great, but ADD demands frequent change, and I was ready for something new. I was already too familiar with the community, which was so Southern: two Baptist churches, a Methodist, and a Presbyterian.

We didn't have a Catholic church, and that might explain my amazement at seeing all the Catholics in the military. When I was explaining to my buddies my limited exposure to Catholics, I'd shock them by saying, "Where I grew up, we thought Catholics and communists were about the same."

• • •

Priests often became my best buds, and I had some funny experiences with them. One happened when I had been in Vietnam for two months and had come to Bien Hoa from up north, where I was stationed with my infantry battalion. I visited the former brigade chaplain, who was now the rear area chaplain. Visiting him was always a good change of pace—we went to the Officers' Club, ate different chow, had a little more peace. He invited me to spend the night in one of the rooms of his hooch, which was luxurious compared to what I was used to.

I was sacking out for the night and got really hungry and rooted around for something to eat. I found some peanut butter, which I love, but no crackers or anything. There were some big white wafers in a jar in the little fridge. I took out about five or six and spread peanut butter on them. They were great even if a little dry, but what the hay, this was Nam. I ate almost all of them, leaving just one or two.

A couple of days later, the brigade chaplain called me in a panic and explained, "I've got a bit of a crisis. Our priest is all shook up. His communion wafers are missing and they had already been consecrated. Any idea what might have happened to them? They were in the refrigerator in the room where you stayed."

"Gee whiz, don't even know what they are."

"You know, big white wafers—they were in a jar."

*Not in his goals but in his transitions,*
*man is great.*
*The most successful leader of all*
*is the one who sees another picture*
*not yet actualized.*

MARY PARKER FOLETT

# Uncle Sam Needs You: From Travis AFB to Saigon—Surreal!

As we wound through the streets of Saigon, which was an alien world, I kept thinking about how easy it would be for someone to throw a grenade into the jeep. I'd heard of it happening, and here were thousands of Vietnamese around us. *Vietnamese!*

Who *were* these people? I hoped the driver knew what he was doing. They were our friends, I guessed, but even then I kept wondering, *How do you tell?* The driver, an experienced chaplain's assistant and an Air Force type, acted like this was everyday fare—he was probably destined to be a taxi driver in New York. Somebody told me it was a joint command, and I didn't have a clue about what a joint command was.

I couldn't comprehend what was going on. We finally came to a fairly modern looking building. MacV headquarters. An acronym. Someone once told me they have a whole room full of civilians at the Pentagon who do nothing but sit around thinking up acronyms for use by the military: MacV—Military Assistance Command, Vietnam. I felt like I was in a twilight zone. We walked up some stairs and into an outer office. A secretary and two more chaplains were there. I think we shook hands. *I was so green.* Then, out came a spit-and-polish guy—a major or maybe a lieutenant colonel chaplain—and he extended his hand and said, "Welcome to Vietnam." *Oh yeah, glad to be here.* "We have your assignments," he said. He flipped through some cards and said, looking at me, "You are going to the 101st Airborne."

It was one of those times when you're hearing something but you're not comprehending it. *No, this couldn't be right,* I thought. *I'm going to Special Forces, that's what everybody had told me. After all, I was trained, one of the few chaplains qualified, had a prefix 3.* I stammered, "I thought I was going to Special Forces." It was as though I had dropped an unmentionable into the punchbowl.

"No—where did you get that?"

"Well, I went through the training."

"Doesn't make any difference," he said. "It's where you are needed. Have you never heard of *needs of the service?* You should be really glad—everybody wants the Screaming Eagles." He said it like he could hardly believe anybody would have the audacity to question such a gift. I was beginning to feel lower than whale manure. How could I not be grateful to go to an infantry unit, one of the best, the Screaming Eagles? I stared at his teeth. They seemed to be full of gold. "Good luck," he said, giving us the brush-off. *Welcome to Vietnam and the Army. God bless America.*

Before I knew it, I was out the door with the other two chaplains. One knew exactly where he was going. He had a great assignment—a chapel and not much action. *I thought that was why we were in Vietnam—action.* I guess it all had to do with definition.

It's amazing: Some people seem to have all the information, and then there are those of us who can't find our feet. It's like college when you start your first class in French or German and there's always someone who knows the vocabulary and can speak the language when you don't even have your book yet! The chapel-bound chaplain looked at me with a kind of smirk and said, "You know what the 101st is called, don't you? The *one-oh-worst!*" He smiled. I should have decked him. He was maybe 10 years older and I could tell he knew a lot, so I let him slide. "Some people call the 101st the puking buzzard." This time he laughed. I know I should have hit him.

Before I knew it, we were heading back to 90th Replacement and then to Bien Hoa to the rear element of the 101st Airborne. Screaming Eagles! The thought suddenly hit me: I'll be able to wear this patch the rest of my Army life on my right shoulder. I mean, we were talking important stuff here—life was grand.

*Think too, of all who suffer*
*as if you shared their pain.*

HEBREWS 13:3,
J. B. PHILLIPS TRANSLATION OF THE BIBLE

# Stop the War, I Want to Get Off

It's hard to describe being in Vietnam. To say I was awed is a serious understatement. We rode into the camp. A big sign said, *Welcome to the 101ˢᵗ Airborne.* People were everywhere, and I had a dreamlike feeling. The smell and heat were almost unbearable. I'll have to say this for the chaplains, they did pretty well at looking after the newcomers. The 101ˢᵗ rear area chaplain was lean and getting ready to leave the country.

I met another chaplain at the Officers' Club one night who was also a cherry and getting ready to go Up North. The O Club held a big significance to me for lots of reasons. This chaplain was a Methodist type who was an entertaining charlatan of the first magnitude—a wheeler-dealer to the max. He was assigned to a battalion in the 3ᵈ Brigade. He lasted just a couple of months—until he got expelled from the country for trying to sell a stolen American Air Force Jeep to some Army guys.

I laugh now to think about it. In fact, I happened to be in the rear area when they kicked him out. He had actually resigned to avoid a court martial, and while he was waiting to go back to the States, he hit three jackpots at the Officers' Club and they expelled him from the Club. Poor guy!

In those days, Officers' Clubs were a part of the social fabric of the military. Usually one had to pay some sort of dues to use the club, and it was a meeting place. Stateside, they were the site of happy hours, gathering spots, or whatever commanders wanted to make of them. But in Vietnam, they represented a kind of respite from the war if you happened to need it. Most of us didn't. We were at war and involved in all that entailed, but on occasion, we'd get the chance to drift in—on the way home or on the way back Up Country.

In a way, an Officers' Club in Nam represented the inequities of life at war. In the rear area and around Bien Hoa and Saigon, some people were living the life of Riley—the best times of their lives—and just up and down the road, men were dying and had none of the amenities many were enjoying routinely. It was weird in a macabre sort of way as well as something that often incensed me.

But I also learned this: the longer I was in-country, the more I realized that there was a great deal of respect for those who were "on the line." You could tell by the boots they wore. "Line doggies" never shined their boots. For one thing, they didn't have rear area "mama sans" to buff them up, but it went beyond that. After being in the rice paddies so long, the boots would turn almost white—the sign of the "grunt."

Despite the respect the grunts earned, the inequities between them and those whose lives were easier always bothered me.

I ran into a sergeant major whose claim to fame was that he stayed in Vietnam for five years. Guess what his job was: He ferried USO shows or made arrangements for their transportation to NCO clubs, mostly in Saigon. This guy lived in the lap of luxury, had a nice little apartment, and great chow all the time. Probably a sweet little Vietnamese woman to look after all his desires. He saved so much money that he was able to return to Atlanta, build a beautiful house, and pay cash for it. While he was doing all this hazardous duty—driving around the lovelies performing in shows—GIs were dying! I'm sure that when he told me about his job, I couldn't get past my disdain.

*Whether regarding the Vietnam war, America's cold war assassinations, or our misguided former alliance with Saddam Hussein, American officials keep their eyes fixed on the future. They rarely admit responsibility for failure, for costly meddling or for large-scale human suffering. They resist debate—internally or publicly—on how good intentions went astray. And they most certainly don't apologize to those harmed.*

SAMANTHA POWER,
*A PROBLEM FROM HELL: AMERICA AND THE AGE OF GENOCIDE*

# You Have Been Selected from Among Your Friends and Neighbors

On my wedding day in 1963, I received my draft notice. I wasn't too shaken up, as I knew that I could get out of it. Almost anybody with any smarts could. Actually, I had a deferment for school but had failed a couple of times, was reinstated, but had not kept my draft board informed. But I wasn't worried. (To be honest, I don't think the notice actually said, *You have been selected from among your friends and neighbors.*)

The truth of the matter, however, is that during the good old days of conscription, the draft had to be taken into consideration. It was an element added to your life that you had to deal with—pure and simple. You either had to go in, which didn't seem too great an idea for many, or get out of it in various ways. In any case, the draft loomed large on your horizon. Not necessarily a bad thing for a youngster, as it did provide an option: When you couldn't do anything else or didn't know what you wanted to do, you could always go into the military. When we had the draft, there was a free pass with youngsters who hung around the street corners or bragged about their lack of direction but didn't truly believe it. For some, there was no choice—they had to do something and the draft made it a little more palatable. I didn't want to get out of the draft, but I didn't think they drafted ministers.

The chaplain recruitment brochure described the great ministry possibilities of the chaplaincy. True! You have a parish called a battalion. There are a thousand men, more or less, in your community. I've often wondered why more clergy don't opt for the military. For most, it is basically a lack of understanding of what ministry in the military is all about. Most who are averse to becoming chaplains usually have such odd ideas about it—everything from thinking that chaplains get their sermons from the Pentagon to not being willing to make the sacrifices—and there are sacrifices. Once you're on the inside, other things come into play, like the chaplain being accepted as a part of the fabric of the military. In fact, many female chaplains say that the military is the one place they don't always have to prove themselves.

The military, like any large institution, is a giant bureaucracy. By the very nature of the modern volunteer military, it must promote itself. It uses Madison Avenue-type marketing strategies such as plastering *Army of One* on the uniforms of race car drivers and their cars. Why would they do that? For one thing, research shows that people who like to watch car racing have the potential for volunteering for the military. They're viewed as less sophisticated and less educated, possibly with positive feelings toward patriotism and an attraction to military life. The Army doesn't advertise at the opera. Let's face it, working class kids made up the military in the sixties just as they do today. As will become abundantly clear, I'm not much on the volunteer Army philosophy.

We didn't have an equitable and fair draft during the Vietnam era. Today we have no draft at all, and we have an incredibly immoral situation, from my standpoint. We have an army of other people's children fighting America's wars.

I have always been an advocate of the draft—or some sort of universal service. September 11 was a great chance for us to promote universal service among America's youth, and we let it escape us. Americans—adults and kids alike—responded to the tragedy, and we ignored the opportunity to provide kids a chance to give back. *Giving back ought to be a given.*

Obviously, I didn't have these opinions when I was on my way to Vietnam, and I certainly was not sophisticated about what I was getting into. I was a preacher in uniform, and now I was going to war. My joke again and again through the years was that I had just started wearing shoes, and suddenly, here I was in the Army and at war. It was all very strange and convoluted.

Getting into the Army should have been a snap when you think of the need. But, it was typical bureaucracy—paperwork up to your eyeballs. The civilian in charge of endorsing was a World War II type—a former chaplain. Endorsement is the process by which the denomination approves you. This guy was one of those people who probably went to some school or seminar and was told how grand it was to remember names. Over the years I got a kick out of him because every time I saw him, he acted like he knew me, but he really didn't know me from Adam's house cat. "It is so good to see you. We appreciate what you are doing for our country," he'd say.

*Resolve to perform what you ought;*
*perform without fail what you resolve.*

BEN FRANKLIN

# Let the War Begin

I spent one night in the chaplain's hooch in the rear at Bien Hoa and then headed "Up North," which was the euphemism for going to war. The division chaplain was at Camp Eagle, my first stop. The division chaplain is usually a lieutenant colonel and is the head of all the chaplains in the division. I had to take a C130 to get to Camp Eagle and landed at Phu Bai. *Phu Bai's all right* became one of those expressions that becomes embedded in your brain forever. I could meet a vet anyplace, anytime, who had been stationed somewhere in the area of Phu Bai and say, *Phu Bai's all right* and I'd get a smile.

The C130, in addition to being pretty scary, had to be about the worst ride I'd ever had. We were crowded in like sardines. I actually had a seat, some straps really, along the edge of the plane, but I felt guilty for even these poor accommodations.

I had a little problem with the officer thing. It was sometimes difficult being an officer ministering to enlisted men. Whether they accepted me—someone who outranked them—as their minister or confidant was mainly up to them. Later in my career, I suggested that the system be changed so that chaplains had no rank. My suggestion was ignored, of course. The military is pretty intractable, and at the top levels, the chaplaincy is often even worse. The chaplaincy in Vietnam days—and now, for that matter—did not discuss issues like changing paradigms and is certainly not likely to in the future. Books like *Who Moved My Cheese* (a good book about organizational change) are not high on the chaplain reading list.

• • •

There were some Vietnamese on the flight, bunched up in the middle of the plane. There were a few old women dressed as though they had just come from a rice paddy—no shoes and black teeth from chewing betel nuts. I don't know why they were on the plane, but with my Southern upbringing I wanted to give a woman my seat. I tried but finally gave up as nobody moved.

We landed at Phu Bai—or, I should say, smashed into the ground. This was no United flight. Phu Bai was to be much of my existence and a little bit of a break as I became a seasoned soldier—we always had to go Phu Bai to go South. The field hospital was there, and I visited it about once a week to see my wounded troops. Thinking about my first trip back to Phu Bai still makes me grin. I came back to pick up thousands of kosher sausages. A rabbi had ordered enough, it seemed, for the world population of

Jews. The poor rabbi's C130 blew up in midair as it had been accidentally filled with JP4 jet fuel, which was a no-no. Since we had no available rabbi, somebody else had to get the sausages. I was volunteered. I can tell you this: the GIs truly enjoyed those kosher sausages and many said, "This almost persuades me to be Jewish."

The division chaplain was a tall, gaunt-looking guy, but he seemed nice. I didn't have a clue as to what all these people did other than the fact that they had been around a while and had rank. I had been to the Basic Chaplain's Course, designed to teach a chaplain basic soldiering skills—marching for instance. What is etched in my old gray matter is how serious many of the older chaplains took the military. Career was already a heavy issue with them—things like promotion, officer efficiency reports, and assignments. I didn't get it. From day one I had always thought that I wanted the military experience and my picture in uniform. After that, I was out of there. I already had the picture, so I figured I'd finish Vietnam and move on out.

I logged a few minutes with the division chaplain, and then he had to go to a meeting. The building we were in was a tent, but it had plywood up around the sides, and there were maps on the wall. I discovered that plywood was a big commodity in Nam. If you had plywood to use or trade, you were the cat's meow. Anyway, there seemed to be plenty. Another chaplain took over when the division chaplain left. He was a little pudgy and had a red face. "Welcome to Vietnam and the 101st," he said. "You're being assigned to the 1/501st in Second Brigade. The chaplain has already DEROSed (date expected to rotate from overseas)." I tried to act like I knew what he meant. "They've been in lots of heavy stuff and I can't really say what's going on now. Your brigade chaplain will be here shortly to pick you up. He'll fill you in. So just relax."

*Oh great, I'll relax.* He left and I wandered outside. As far as my eyes could see, there were tents and men coming and going. Everybody had a gun—sorry, a weapon. Never say *gun* in the military. It's a *weapon!* Here's a joke: A trainee calls a weapon a gun. A sergeant grabs the weapon and says, "This is for killing." Then he grabs his privates and says, "Son, this is a gun." With his other hand he raises the weapon and says, "This is for killing" and then places his hand on his privates again and says, "This is for fun."

The entrance to Camp Eagle always amazed me. Outside the gates were entrepreneurial Vietnamese with little makeshift shops. A GI could get almost anything he wanted—such as a tattoo, which I was always a little sorry I never got. It seems that every 101st trooper had the eagle logo on his shoulder with a banner underneath that said, AIRBORNE. Below that were the words GOD AND MOTHER or something on that order. I was also fascinated with the sandals the Vietnamese made out of old tires—GOOD FOR FIFTY THOUSAND MILES OR THE LIFE OF YOUR FEET.

• • •

The brigade chaplain showed up. His face was red, which made me wonder if he wasn't hitting the sauce a little. The other thing I noticed was that he was a little overweight. How could someone be overweight in Vietnam? But he was a nice guy and had been around the airborne for a long time. He had a star on his wings and a wreath around the star—a master blaster. We got into his jeep and took off. I noticed that we had two weapons in the back and he was wearing a forty-five. I hadn't thought much about weapons, but I remembered that in chaplain school someone had said, "The chaplain does not carry a weapon," and then a long debate had ensued.

I learned quickly that a chaplain *does* need a weapon. Not for *his* protection, but so GIs will feel comfortable when the chaplain is in the field. I discovered this when I was in the field, unarmed, and the grunt I was with obviously felt protective toward me, but it was obvious that he couldn't be worried about me—he needed to be concerned with himself and his buddy. To do otherwise was to put himself in jeopardy. Life is too short and tenuous in the boonies not to be fully alert and aware.

So I became a good soldier. I was a country boy, raised on a farm with guns and hunting. In some ways, war became a game—to seek out the enemy, hunt him, find him or outwit him. I don't mean to trivialize the seriousness of what we were doing. But this was a guerilla war, and the winners were not the ones with the most firepower but the ones who were the most cunning hunters.

*When Dorothy and her little dog, Toto, are swept away from Kansas in a wild tornado, they end up in the magical land of Oz. Soon Dorothy is off to meet the powerful Wizard of Oz, the only one who can get her and Toto back home. On the way to meet the Wizard, she meets the Scarecrow, the Tin Man, and the Cowardly Lion, who join her on the yellow brick road to the Emerald City, the Wizard's home. Only the Wizard, they think, can grant them their wishes—that the Scarecrow might get a brain, the Tin Man a heart, and the Cowardly Lion courage. And the big question is, will Dorothy and Toto ever see home again?*

# This Ain't Kansas, Toto

The trip from Camp Eagle to LZ Sally took an hour or so, depending on the traffic, which was not a lot different from traffic in the San Francisco Bay area or any other big city. There were military vehicles, Vietnamese walking, bicycles everywhere, and a few scooters mixed in. Each scooter seem to hold about three generations of people. Our driver did his best to dodge the potholes, but on occasion the entire vehicle sank down into a gigantic fissure gouged into the road. When he hit one straight on, it rattled our teeth.

We went through the outskirts of Hue, the old imperial city. The 1968 Tet offensive was a significant turning point in the Vietnam war, as most who have studied the era will attest, and Hue was a big part of that tumultuous time. One of my best buddies told me that he can remember traveling through Hue just before Tet and seeing strange-looking men in formal uniforms. Later on he discovered that they were North Vietnamese regulars—and it was not quite time to start the Vietnamese New Year.

As for me, I thought it was a gorgeous city, and I marveled at the people, especially the schoolgirls—they wore beautiful long one-piece dresses, cut up the thigh but not revealing. And they stepped out smartly.

It was this initial trip that set the tone for my time in Vietnam. We were pretty somber as we pulled onto the highway leaving Hue. It already seemed like I'd been in Vietnam forever, but it had been just three weeks. At eight in the morning, the heat was already oppressive.

There was a street to the right. It, too, was jammed with military vehicles, scooters, peasants walking with huge loads on their heads, and lots of buses. Traffic weaved around potholes and miraculously moved forward. We were leaving behind a marketplace that had filled my nostrils with the pungent aromas of half-raw fish mixed with vegetables, slaughtered meat, squid, and other Vietnamese delectables. I eventually got to where I could eat all of them.

As we'd passed the marketplace, we'd picked up another vehicle heading to Sally. We came to a "T" in the road. To the right was QL551, a secondary highway neatly dotted with GI bunkers between the road and the Perfume River. I would be logging in lots of time on that road to the beach. To the left was a road leading along the river to more of the city. We turned left. For me, these were strange sights in a beautiful city. Remnants of the war abounded, mostly due to the Tet offensive.

Tet was a push for North Vietnam's victory and it awakened those few Americans who still paid attention to Vietnam. It was a news media extravaganza, even though reporters got most of it wrong. The North Vietnamese took countless heavy casualties, but the media made it look like they were the victors.

About twenty girls, probably university students, who were dressed for the most part in yellow *ao dais*, strode briskly past the intersection as we momentarily stopped. We turned right, crossed the Perfume River, and broke out into the country. LZ Sally was about five miles due west of Hue, along a road even worse than the one we'd been traveling.

Base camps existed for logistical purposes, and were peopled with brigades of three to five thousand men. From those enclaves sprang fire support bases, which were usually occupied by battalion-size units of 750 to 1000 men plus support units. We were heading to Sally, our base camp.

We passed peasants buried up to their ankles in water-soaked rice fields. Life was going on in Vietnam. War was nothing new to them. What did it matter?—Frenchmen, Americans, all the same. For them, this was the American war. I stared at them. In my mind rang one constant question: *What have I gotten myself into?* This all seemed so fanatical. A thought ran across a corner of my mind: *I don't know much about Vietnam.* For years, I'd heard about Vietnam, but didn't really know anything about their history; their invasions. Strange—we were in a foreign country riding through fields of farmers in rice paddies. What was wrong with this picture?

We slowed to a stop. "Are we there?" I said to the brigade chaplain. "Naw, looks like the bridge is out and we've got to go around." The other jeep was ahead of us, and it made sense for us to just go around them and let their jeep follow us. But we didn't—the jeep ahead backed up and started across the ditch beside the bridge. The next thing I knew there was a horrendous explosion. In what looked and felt like slow motion, their jeep was picked up and thrown into the air. It turned over and those inside tumbled out.

"What happened?" someone screamed.

There was shocked silence for what seemed like minutes, and then someone said, "I think somebody blew us up." It was forever before people started collecting themselves. Later on, I must have instinctively run to the jeep, which was probably not all that smart. It had been blown into three or four pieces—the carnage was unreal. I hesitate to describe it, but still remember it clearly, many years later. I saw a soldier's left arm, which was severed from his body, and his left leg, which was shredded up to the thigh. There was no doubt he was dead. The brigade chaplain's face was ashen, and he said over and over, "Oh, Jesus." Now, as I think about it, this was a very appropriate comment.

This was my first introduction to the VC—the Vietcong. They had booby-trapped the makeshift path for vehicles at the side of the bridge because they knew we'd use it when we couldn't cross the bridge. Two people were dead—the driver of the jeep and a PFC riding with him.

A helicopter appeared carrying medics. Next came a "dust-off" or "slick" (another helicopter) to pick up the dead. We'd see them more frequently than we'd like in months to come. An engineer team arrived to sweep the road for more bombs.

"They're all your enemies," an NCO told me when I first came into the country. Maybe they are, I thought, as I looked at these four medics putting the remains of a soldier into a rubber bag. I felt sick.

*It really is a wonder that I haven't dropped all my ideals because they seem so absurd and impossible to carry out. Yet I keep them, because in spite of everything, I still believe that people are really good at heart. I simply can't build up my hopes on a foundation consisting of confusion, misery, and death. I see the world gradually being turned into a wilderness. I hear the ever approaching thunder, which will destroy us too. I can feel the sufferings of millions and yet, if I look up into the heavens, I think that it will come right, that this cruelty too will end, and peace and tranquility will return again.*

ANNE FRANK

# Been to Hell, Lived to Tell

(inscribed on a Zippo lighter from Nam)

An Army captain arrived to survey the ghastly scene and escort us on into Sally. To say that I was on edge as we drove the last couple of miles would be an understatement. You know how it is when you just don't feel right—your heart is racing, you've had too much coffee, you're fretting, and you think the other shoe is about to drop. This was how I felt, and I wasn't to be disappointed.

Just as Sally came into sight, a VC opened up with an AK-47. At first it sounded like distant fire crackers, but the jeep slammed to a halt and we scrambled outside. "Some mother messing with us," somebody said. Unfortunately— or fortunately, based on one's perspective—all of this was making me into a real soldier. It happened, and it was survival.

Many memories—funny, serious, or embarrassing— come flooding in as I write this, and a couple are directly related to the AK-47.

One was when I decided to play hero and stopped and arrested a Vietnamese man in Hue for carrying one. It turned out that the people in the city played by different rules than those in the field. In the field, humping the boonies, nobody was supposed to have AKs, and anybody with one was fair game—they were the enemy. So here I was in the city, playing hero. After some hollering and screaming and a standoff, an American MP who happened to be riding by stopped and took charge. Later on, I discovered that if we had arrested or shot everybody in Hue who had an AK, we would pretty much have annihilated the population. I was pretty embarrassed.

The AK made a startling popping sound so distinctive that once you heard it a few times, especially in combat, you knew to duck, get down, run, whatever you needed to do, just like that first day.

There was always lots of bantering back and forth about which was the better weapon—the Russian-made

AK-47 or the M16. I thought the M16 was better, not that I had all that much experience. The AK could fire almost under almost any conditions—in water, wherever. Those who liked the M16 said that it was the far superior weapon if you kept it clean. If not, it often jammed.

The M16 bullet was also supposed to be more deadly when penetrating the body. When the AK slug penetrates a body, if it doesn't hit vital organs, a flesh wound results. With the M16, the bullet's spinning motion rips up the victim's insides.

A new doctor came into the battalion; he was a great guy, but I guess he was never briefed or didn't have the field time to know what the sound of an AK would do to troops. He was a Southerner who loved weapons, and almost right off the bat he began to acquire a few collectables—I don't have a clue what he was going to do with the AKs in particular. One day, he went out to the edge of the Fire Support Base and did a little target practice with the AK. The moment they heard that familiar pop, troops started laying down fire, and the artillery battery was ready to light him up before someone discovered it was the doc.

*I have seen most of these events.*
*Those I haven't have been told by the old*
*warriors, who talk of such things around*
*poker games, over beers, or when they're*
*alone and think no one is listening. These*
*are secrets, forged in the hot fires of combat,*
*pressed on the soul like a medal,*
*and polished years later—*
*still gleaming, still hurting.*

JOHN P. MCAFEE, AUTHOR OF THE VIETNAM NOVEL
*SLOW WALK IN A SAD RAIN*

# Fear—The Great Equalizer

Once we finally got inside Sally, we wound our way around rows of tents to the brigade chaplain's office. It was a two-room affair, and he immediately disappeared for about 30 minutes. I think he was visiting with his friend Jim (Beam). When he returned, he kept rattling on about covering the troops, where to stay, and how best to do it. I don't mean to disparage him, but he seemed distracted, and he was sweating profusely. In a sense, who wouldn't be after what we'd been through? Later on, I surmised that it was fear that made him so distracted.

A helicopter pilot told me a story about how he was flying the brigade chaplain somewhere and, for a joke, someone hit the floor of the aircraft several times. The chaplain thought somebody was shooting, and he cowered in the corner. Give me a break—that was a pretty cruel joke. As I was to come to know later, he spent most of his time in his tent, almost to the point of seclusion. In fact, it became somewhat of a problem, and I ended up attempting a rescue. Even in the Nam, there were always meetings and briefings that the chaplain was supposed to attend. Not that he had anything to contribute or that anybody paid him any attention, but he was a member of the staff.

Marginalizing of the chaplain's role always ticked me off. We went to meetings and had something to say, but usually it was discounted or trivialized. But who knows—maybe we imagined it because we felt inadequate. Mainly, I think, it had to do with our own emotions and feelings of displacement—*What am I doing here!* How incongruent the chaplain's presence is among all these war fighters—a man of peace, prepared to talk constantly about the Prince of Peace. The concept seemed a little out of kilter, as we say in North Carolina.

The brigade chaplain missed staff meetings more often than not. For some reason, at one meeting his absence became noticeable and the brigade commander sent someone to fetch him. He was inebriated—big trouble.

His fear drove him to drink, I think. Or, maybe it didn't—maybe he was usually somewhat weird but became even stranger in Nam. Or, possibly, he could have been like many GIs, who brought a problem to Vietnam and war exacerbated it. He was from a very conservative, alcohol-abstaining church, so drinking was definitely prohibited. Add his feelings of guilt for having a drinking problem to his fear, and he had something to deal with.

His behavior became such a problem that it appeared he would be shipped home. In a frantic call, he asked if he could visit me. Sure, I said. It was such a mess as we tried to dry him out for two or three weeks. Fortunately, he had to go home on an emergency leave because of a family problem, and he never returned.

Vietnam affected everyone, even chaplains, in different ways. I'm not sure it has been different in other wars. Some chaplains saw Vietnam as a great opportunity for ministry and others, despite their best motives, simply could not operate in an environment of danger—a place where they had to create and interpret. It was no easy ministry!

Some chaplains thrive in a war environment while others crash and burn; still others simply make it, a day at a time—feeling that it's a prison sentence until they're out of there. Fortunately, I was in the first category. I loved doing ministry in Vietnam.

Fear brings out strange behavior in people. The longer people were in-country, the more cautious they became—as if they knew they were closing in on the end of their tour and they had to be extra careful. Guys in the field would almost refuse to go on patrol in the last few days. It was an unwritten rule that a guy could go to the rear—at least to the battalion or brigade headquarters—when he got down to his last few days.

There were such inequities in Nam. On the line, we were always humping the boonies (staying in the field). We'd go for months and literally not have a real stand-down (rest)—never go in to the fire support base or go to Sally or, heaven help us, get lush duty guarding the bridges. In movies like *Hamburger Hill* that showcased the 101st, you'd think soldiers were sitting around villages with prostitutes or smoking pot—leisure activity. No way! Some REMFs maybe, but not my unit. (REMF means rear echelon m—f—. I often thought that if the F-word were banned, the Nam warrior's vocabulary would be reduced significantly.)

Our troops were in the field most of the time. I once saw a statistic that compared the amount of combat time for Vietnam soldiers with that of World War II soldiers. It showed that World War II soldiers saw combat something like 45 days a year while those in Vietnam saw 200. I don't know about the World War II soldiers, but I can tell you this: few days passed when soldiers in my unit didn't take fire or become involved in some kind of enemy activity. Combat soldiers were always on edge—something was always about to happen. Does that take a toll on a person? You'd better believe it—a big-time toll. It's like sitting on the edge of your seat, preparing for a crash, and getting gut-wrenching news that you know is coming. It's mind-boggling to always be on edge. Did we get used to it? No. The large numbers of PTSD (post-traumatic stress disorder) cases we see from Vietnam is understandable—the toll of combat is incalculable.

*I've never met a person, I don't care what his condition, in whom I could not see possibilities. I don't care how much a man may consider himself a failure, I believe in him, for he can change the thing that is wrong in his life any time he is ready and prepared to do it. Whenever he develops the desire, he can take away from his life the thing that is defeating it. The capacity for reformation and change lies within.*

PRESTON BRADLEY

# The Brooklyn of Vietnam

In every branch of the Army, there's a course you must attend after you've been in the service for a few years. The chaplains' course was located at Fort Hamilton in Brooklyn, New York. Describing LZ Sally, the brigade headquarters, is like trying to describe Brooklyn. It can't be done. As a young captain attending the chaplains' course after Vietnam, one of Brooklyn's neighborhoods, Flatbush Avenue, reminded me very much of Sally—all of these people eating at ethnic restaurants, doing things, making moves with no real purpose, and yet it all had purpose. At Sally I'd see soldiers moving like ants, hooches, cardboard, plywood, tents large and small, and signs everywhere. Out of this world. We wound around through roads and paths and got to where we were going. I was in a daze.

Every battalion maintained a small administration section at the brigade headquarters. Out from there was the battalion fire support base, where all the companies operated. It was very confusing, but I hoped to be a fast learner.

I didn't log in much time at the brigade or battalion rear at Sally other than to write letters of condolence. In the early days, the chaplain wrote a letter to the parents of each soldier killed. This was a tough thing for me to do because I took it so personally. We had an adjutant who was constantly telling me, "You can't take it personal. It is a job, something you have to do. Get it done and move on." If I knew the soldier personally, I tried to put in something special. If I didn't, I made something up. I labored over each one and got farther and farther behind until everybody in the admin section was waiting for me—they needed to put a check mark on their to-do list.

I finally had to give up and write form letters. They were all typed individually, and if I knew the person, I insisted on writing a different sentence or two. Writing these letters was a very emotional experience and plagued me my entire time in Nam. I should have done more. I should have done better. These families were hurting and

I should have been relieving the pain. It was my job and I wasn't doing it.

I learned some lessons about grief. A combat death— when someone is killed in combat, killed by the enemy— does something to loved ones left behind. They want to know how the person died. *Did he suffer? What did people say about him?* I remember the family of a young lieutenant who had been with us only a short time. Tall, handsome, a Catholic—great guy. Green as grass and reluctant to do anything lest he mess up. I remember him as incredibly introspective, which is the worst thing to be in Vietnam. After a while, most GIs learn to just *do it*—don't think or contemplate; it will drive you crazy. This lieutenant played the guitar and sometimes played a song before our worship service. He really wasn't all that good a guitarist, somebody told me, but I thought he was grand.

His platoon got into an awful firefight and he was killed. I sent his folks the standard letter to which I added a brief comment that he sometimes played the guitar for me. They wrote back with questions. I wrote with some answers. Other members of the family wrote. I answered. More questions and finally the grief and futility and waste of a loved one came through and I no longer knew what to say. I stopped writing but have always felt bad about my lack of courage.

*Grief is a tidal wave that overtakes you,*
*smashes down upon you with unimaginable*
*force, sweeps you up into its darkness,*
*where you tumble and crash against*

> *unidentifiable surfaces only to be thrown*
> *out on an unknown beach, bruised,*
> *reshaped. Grief makes what others think*
> *of you moot. It shears away the masks of*
> *normal life and forces brutal honesty out of*
> *your mouth before propriety can stop you.*
> *It shoves away friends and scares away so-*
> *called friends, and rewrites your address*
> *book for you.*
>
> STEPHANIE ERICSSON,
> *COMPASSION THROUGH THE DARKNESS*

My first night at Sally was memorable. My assistant was on R and R (rest and relaxation), someone told me. I had considered waiting around until he returned, but I wanted to get to the war. The assistant had a great reputation as a soldier, and this was comforting.

I shared a tent at Sally with men who I eventually discovered were the cooks. In my side of the tent were a small cot, a little field desk, and a generator-powered light. Pretty standard fare. A plywood partition separated my part of the tent from the other, much larger, part where the mess hall cooks lived. I still smile when I think about my introduction to them. I was convinced that I had entered some netherworld—a twilight zone. About dark I heard voices jabbering incessantly in a language I didn't recognize.

Sometime after midnight, I heard these voices again. Occasionally could I make out something that sounded like English—usually M—F—. It made me laugh when I caught on. The term *Ebonics* had not yet entered the lexicon, but I finally realized that I was listening to the GI language of African American soldiers. The stories, what little I could make out, were really something. First they filleted whitie in general; then the commander; the VC; Vietnam; women, both foreign and domestic; and each other. I'd like to include a little of the dialogue, but I don't think I could do it justice. It was funny, verbose, awful, sickening, and enlightening. It was all there in the cooks' tent! They must have gone on all night or close to it, because if I slept a wink, I don't remember it. The next morning I was like a zombie. It was blistering hot and I was praying for daylight.

What always amazed me, even at war, was that you had to do paperwork. I filled out the necessary forms— who I wanted notified in case I bought the farm; how much money I wanted to receive each month, etc. I should have given a little more thought to the forms. Who *should* be notified in case of death or emergency? Way down the road, I got banged up a bit, nothing anywhere close to life-threatening, but I bled, so I must have been given a Purple Heart. I didn't know anything about it until much later, but they sent the medal home to Jackie and it scared her to death. The families always suffer with not knowing what's going on with their loved ones at war. I remember my mother, trekking to the mailbox every day when my brother Chuck was in Korea. Of course, I was not around to watch her when I was in Nam, but I'm sure it was just as difficult for her.

Sally was supposed to be in a secure rear area, but sometime before morning, I had encounter two with the enemy. The familiar *varump, varump* was followed by a high-pitched scream that could wake the dead. Then people started running. "Incoming" was shouted over and over by someone as rounds exploded. I saw a barracks-like tent take a direct hit. Wood and men were running and flying, it seemed. I looked for cover, but I'm not sure I ever found it. For what seemed like an hour, the VC lobbed mortars.

Then, just as quickly as it had begun, it stopped. It was over and all was calm, as if nothing had ever happened. I concluded then that I wanted to get to the field. Maybe I was there and this was the way it was going to be. But somehow I felt that someplace else had to be safer. One of the GIs joked the next day, "Chaplain, last night was the first time we've been hit in weeks. It was your welcome to paradise."

*When you go home,*
*tell them of us and say—*
*For your tomorrow,*
*We gave our today.*

EPITAPH ON 2D INFANTRY DIVISION MEMORIAL, BURMA

*I have chosen not to ask why.*
*I don't want to waste what limited energy*
*I have on a question*
*for which I don't think I'll get an answer.*

WIFE OF A YOUNG SOLDIER KILLED IN IRAQ
WHO HAS THREE CHILDREN

# You Are Getting at Least the Bronze [Star]

*Under a hail of enemy and rocket fire* is a phrase that appears on every single award recommendation I've ever read. I was fascinated by hero medals during my time in Vietnam. Sometimes they caused problems. Soldiers didn't seem to care much about them, but to families they mattered a lot. Medals are the military's way of saying "attaboy" (or "attagirl"), but giving and receiving medals was always a little suspect, and I have to admit that I developed an attitude about them.

My usual line was that when you walked by our sister battalion, you could see them lined up three deep getting medals, but in my unit, a soldier would have to bleed a pint to get one. Not true, of course, but that's what it seemed like. Whether someone got a medal had a lot to do with his commander. It seemed like when you deserved one, you didn't get it; when you did something that might be considered heroic, the medal folks were nowhere around.

In the beginning, I didn't know exactly how the medal system worked—how they were awarded or who got them. When I learned the system, I put in lots of guys for medals they deserved. If I didn't know the specific reason they deserved one, I made something up, because I can guarantee it happened at some point. A combat soldier could not spend time in Nam and not be in a situation that deserved a medal. Of course, some people got medals they didn't deserve. I had an XO once who claimed jokingly that a commander he knew got eighteen at one time and his sergeant major got seventeen. After this the XO would laugh heartily and say, "The sergeant major had a bad day."

• • •

Most combat vets I know don't like to talk about their hero status, and for good reasons: (1) Some know that often medals go not to the most deserving but to those who either pursue them or know people who will pursue them on their behalf. (2) Most who have received hero medals have some doubt that they deserve them. (3) Many combat vets are embarrassed when they think they have received something that should rightly go to a dead comrade or to his family. (4) Most combat vets who wear medals on their chests simply don't feel worthy.

So why wear them? Well, medals are an announcement that you've been in combat; that you've met the test and passed. Most Army grunts in Vietnam came under fire everyday—mortared, raked with fire, in constant firefights. This was the nature of being a combat soldier in Vietnam. For most of those Vietnam combat soldiers, there were no medals.

• • •

I finally gave up my views on medals years after Nam. Families prided themselves on the medals—they were tangible proof that the sacrifices of their loved ones were worth it—a recognition that their lives had not been in vain. And, so I supported them the best I could and buried my attitude.

The medal story I like the best is about a young man who was one of McNamara's so-called 100,000. These are the cannon-fodder soldiers who joined the service when standards were lowered, and what we did to them should be a double blight on the conscience of our country, but surely not on those soldiers, many of whom lived and died as true heroes. One man I knew was brave beyond all description and always seemed to be getting a medal, either during a ceremony or when a general impacted him with one. (*Impacted* means that the general gave the medal on the spot and the paperwork was to follow. Most of the time it didn't, but for the moment, the soldier felt recognized—or most did.) This kid told me one day that he had refused a medal.

"Why?" I asked.

"It was not the right color," he said.

"Not the right color?"

He explained that he had plenty of the kind of medals they wanted to give him.

"Which one is that?"

"The Silver Star." (The Silver Star is blue and white, the third highest medal for bravery that can be given. It's a highly coveted award.)

He wanted one of the green ones. The green one is the Army Commendation Medal (ACM), which in Vietnam was mostly given for breathing. I don't mean to disparage the Army Commendation Medal or any other medal, but there's no comparison between the ACM and the Silver Star. I've often thought that one of the reasons that my friend did so well as a combat soldier is that he simply "did"—no thinking or figuring things out. *Do it!*

Many of these guys in McNamara's 100,000, maybe even without realizing it, had a keen appreciation of the opportunities that the military provides. Back home, they might have followed a plow or washed dishes in a local restaurant, if that much. In the Nam, at least, as one told me, they were doing something important. Now, that's "attitude!"

*Vietnam was a mistake.*

McNAMARA

*Duh!!!!!!!!!!!!*

# The Moron Corps

I only recently read about this slang term supposedly used by GIs in Vietnam referring to what is shamefully known as McNamara's 100,000. It was actually more like 354,000. The plan was supposedly hatched by Secretary of Defense McNamara to make President Johnson look good by providing more troops for Vietnam without calling up the Reserves and National Guard.

Most who have written about this shameful and immoral idea view McNamara's 100,000 as a total failure. However, my experience leads me to a different view and in a way, somewhat of a theological truth. Sometimes a perceived moral failure turns out, in the big picture, to have been the best decision. McNamara's 100,000 experiment began with the worst of motives—getting more cannon fodder for Vietnam—yet it ended up empowering a group of America's underclass. I saw many of them soldier with great valor. Not once do I remember hearing another soldier refer to them as the *Moron Corps*. I think this is some journalist's histrionics.

Paradoxically, I think historians/writers like to attach various motives to scenarios, giving them logic when there is no logic. Maybe LBJ didn't want to call up more Reserves and National Guard lest he incur the wrath of the antiwar types. And, given the circumstances and what we now know about McNamara, this devious plan of going into America's ghettos and the rural South for more cannon fodder sounds like something he would do. However, in my experience, what this immoral idea did was to give some forgotten Americans a chance at participating in a slice of history, like it or not. And they truly did participate, as most of them became combat infantrymen.

Was Vietnam better than no chance at all for these men who, had the standards not been lowered, would never have been Nam-bound? I think so. If they died, they may, as my good friend says, "have died in vain, but they lived in honor." And some of them did benefit from training and did escape poverty.

I will never forget going into the wilds of Appalachia once to deliver what we called in Vietnam a "brave eagle." The brave eagle was a little coin that was given to a 101st trooper for killing one of the enemy, and they were much coveted by combat soldiers. This may sound a little gross to some coffee-shop type hanging out in Berkeley, but we were at war, and war is no day at the beach. If this concept rattles someone's sensibilities, so be it.

I promised this trooper that when I got home and settled, I'd bring him his brave eagle. I finally located his place way back in a holler. He was sitting on the porch in his wheel chair when I drove up—no legs. I wanted to cry. The tears were welling up in my eyes. He greeted me with a paratrooper's *HooAhhhhhhhhh* and called me by a term that was one of endearment: "Preacher." As we talked, his mom and dad and a whole gaggle of relatives and locals walked by the porch. I gave him his brave eagle and he said, "Preacher, I'm glad I went to Vietnam. I'm not a whole man, but I've got me a government pension and I can give my folks more than I ever could if I hadn't gone." I wanted to cry and tell him that I didn't care what the government gave him, they could never repay him for what he'd lost. I didn't.

He named about a half dozen guys he was with when his whole squad was hit and mostly killed. He pulled out a packet of letters he'd gotten from families and a few from some of his buddies. It was meaningful. Yes, good coming from a bad—even immoral—idea!

*Beware of these experts in religion,*
*for they love to parade in dignified robes*
*and to be bowed to by the people*
*as they walk along the street.*
*And they love the seats of honor in the*
*synagogues and at religious festivals!*
*But even while they are praying long*
*prayers with great outward piety,*
*they are planning schemes*
*to cheat widows out of their property.*
*Therefore God's heaviest sentence*
*awaits these men.*

LUKE 20:46-47

# "We Were Wrong— We Were Terribly Wrong!"

Give me a break! McNamara's revelation of Vietnam being a mistake still irritates me. I can understand his quest for some sort of redemption, but this doesn't resonate with me or most of the public, based on their reaction. It is true that when we are immersed in an event, we often can't see it. And hindsight is 20/20. Still, his "We were wrong—we were terribly wrong!" doesn't cut it.

It makes me think about those brave young troops who paid the ultimate price in Nam and those who are still paying it. What I remember about McNamara and all the VIPs coming to Vietnam was the princely treatment they received. They stayed in plush hotels—with servants—red carpet all the way. Westmoreland played midday tennis and required a perfectly poached egg. This ticks me off to the max. America's young men were living and dying just miles away while McNamara and Westmoreland and their legions were living in the lap of luxury. Don't think the same things aren't happening today.

A few times I went into Saigon, and once I ate at a floating restaurant, as it was called. Sitting there, the war seemed a long way away. When I was out in some rice paddy with the troops and getting angry, I often tried to imagine the generals sitting at that same floating restaurant or at the Rex Hotel. I imagined them dining on white tablecloths watching the distant artillery and rockets exploding—with the occasional tracer rounds and flares thrown in for good measure. I wouldn't have been surprised if they had called the waiter over to complain that the thousand-pound bombs were drowning out the sound of the orchestra.

• • •

I was being assigned to the 1st of the 501st Infantry battalion of the 101st Airborne. I had known that, but when my war was over, I would feel a lot of pride in being in this unit.

For now, though, I was tired, shook up and ready to get on with it.

The 1/501 was the original parachute battalion of the Army. What a history! And the father of the airborne, General William C. Lee, the first commander of the 101<sup>st</sup> Airborne Division, was from my hometown. I grew up walking past a plaque that told the brief story of the airborne and his part in it. What an amazing coincidence, which I surely didn't realize in Nam.

We were the Geronimo battalion. Nobody had a clue how it came to be called that, Geronimo being an Indian chief. I learned the reason eventually, not in Nam but later on, when I authored the biography of General Lee—one of America's true unsung heroes. In doing the research, I discovered that when the original group was training to be paratroopers, one night on the way home from a local tavern, one of them bragged that instead of shouting the traditional *thousand one, thousand two, thousand three* after jumping out of the  airplane (which was the time it took for the parachute to deploy) he would shout out *Geronimo*. Well, he did and the lore began.

Not that it made any real difference to guys fighting in Nam. The VC could care less that you were a member of the first parachute battalion of the U. S. Army.

*In war everything is the norm.*
*I have spoken to brave men who have had*
*hysterics on the battlefield, who have run*
*from the enemy, who have left their friends*
*to die in the heat of battle.*
*I have had revealed to me the things of*
*which you cannot even begin to dream.*
*I tell you, my friend, war is hell, but*
*take heart. When a soldier goes to war,*
*everything is pre-forgiven.*

SPOKEN BY A PSYCHIATRIST
IN THE BOOK *WORD OF HONOR,* BY NELSON DEMILLE

# Finally, I'm at the War— Geronimo!

The helicopter picked me up at Sally about ten o'clock (ten hundred hours as the military would say), along with five other replacements. We were going to a fire support base called Mongoose. It was my first helicopter ride. Another first in air travel for me. The first time I rode in an airplane, I jumped out of it. I was from a small town and my world pretty much revolved around a landscape that didn't cover much territory.

From the sky, the patchwork quilt below was incredible. The rice paddies were very distinctive and beautiful and the country was a bright green. I wondered what was going on down below. My life was entering the world of war—one that was unusual in every sense of the word— Quang Tri, Hi-Lang, and Thua Thien Province would enter my vocabulary.

I was scared, or maybe excited. I looked around at the other five men and smiled. They were stone-faced and as shook up as I was. They looked so young. The average age of the Vietnam soldier was about 18. I was an old man of 27. I had finished college and seminary and had a year in the Army. These guys should have been going to college, chasing girls, or driving fast cars, but not going to war. I didn't think of that then but I do now.

(I'm writing this chapter at Christmastime and just saw a hokey TV special. A young soldier is killed in Iraq. His family cannot recover from his death, and they are visited by the dead son in disguise and he helps them deal with their grief—a good story, but it's TV, where they can make anything happen—if only this really could happen to families in grief due to war. At the end, in his final appearance to the family, the disguised son makes an observation to himself: *Yes, I went to war and did my duty, but is the world any safer?*)

I will never forget those five guys in the helicopter, the looks on their faces, the silence, and the noise and wind. Too noisy to talk, so I prayed. *Dear God, please help us all.*

*Let this year pass fast. Let all of us be on this helicopter on the way out of Nam before we know it. Amen.*

I wish I could have kept up with these guys. More than 35 years later, I still wonder about them. Vietnam may be like any experience that is life-changing—you can only think about it in retrospect, and I have been thinking about it ever since I was there. At the time, I never seriously thought about whether the war was right or wrong. In the years to come, I have confronted the meaning and, in a sense, the geopolitical aspect of Nam with great regularity through books and through documentaries like *Fog of War*.

It's amazing what retrospect can do. In a symbolic sense, I left a part of me—my soul—in Vietnam. I think I mirrored the conservative thinking of the day. Protesters and others who opposed the war were playing into the Communists' hands. As I look back on it now, I wish I could have been involved in Vietnam with my present head but my then body. It was way over my head at the time!

Since I have ADD, it's hard to know how much Vietnam has added to my inability to focus. My wife says that if I couldn't blame things on Vietnam and ADD, what would I do? She's joking, I hope. But for me, it was a war fought in a mist, and I saw it through a glass darkly with the Biblical concept of the light to come.

I didn't think in terms of protesters being communists, and I had not thought of the rightness or wrongness of the war. It simply had to do with duty, although to be honest, I probably hadn't thought that through either. I have now. Mostly, it has to do with what I consider revisionist history: a kind of equating those who were dodging the draft with those who may have been honestly protesting the war or those who got deferments with soldiers who went to Vietnam. The American soldiers of Vietnam did their duty. Dodging the draft and protesting the war on the "mean" streets of Berkeley, California, is not the same as dodging bullets in Vietnam!

I've read many of the theories of our involvement in Vietnam and have often quoted a comment Billy Graham made early on about our involvement. "In the beginning," he said, "it was a moral decision: keeping a big country from taking over a smaller one." This made sense to me. It was only later that I came to understand a little of the politics of both America and Vietnam. The corruptness of the South Vietnamese government and our own decisions that were simply wrongheaded or stupid played a part.

Even though I didn't think it then, maybe it was in my psyche somewhere that we shouldn't have gone to Vietnam at all, but since we did, let's do what we need to do to win the war and get out. This obviously was a simplistic view of a young man who hadn't bothered to think it through. It really wouldn't have made any difference if I had. Only hindsight produces complex and often profound views.

*We few, we happy few,*
*we band of brothers.*
*For me, today,*
*who sheds his blood with me*
*shall be my brother.*

WILLIAM SHAKESPEARE, MADE POPULAR
IN THE TV MOVIE *BAND OF BROTHERS,*
ECHO COMPANY, 101ST AIRBORNE, WWII

# Let's Get This War Rolling

At the end of the ride from Sally, the helicopter landed in the stifling heat. It's hard to describe the picture once you're on the ground. The tents were spread out in a big, tight "T"—a long, gigantic bunker built into the ground. There were a couple of GP (general purpose) medium-size tents at one end of a little tiny pathway. The chopper had landed on perforated steel pads— PSP they were called. The six of us stood around for a little bit and finally a specialist 4 came from somewhere and said, "OK, you cherries, come with me." Then he saw me and said, "Chaplain, we didn't expect you." He hesitated for a moment, then pointed and said, "There's your tent."

Sure enough, there was a little cross flying from a pole. At least I had a tent. And the Son of Man had "no place to lay his head."

I quickly found out that life in Vietnam exemplified the adage someone told me early on: "In the military, if you don't look after yourself, nobody else is going to do it for you." Being self-reliant would hold me in good stead throughout my military career, and more importantly, it put me in a position to be able to look after other soldiers. There's a saying: "There's nothing too good for soldiers, and that's what they get—nothing." This really is not true, as there are lots of things in place for the soldier. However, the military, like any big bureaucracy, is often geared to doing the least it can. In some ways, the chaplain's job is to make sure that individual soldiers don't get lost in the maze. I always saw myself as a crusading advocate for the soldier—making sure the system didn't steamroll over him.

I hated it when chaplains didn't do their jobs. Many spent more time looking after their own stuff than they did taking care of the troops. It reminds me of the present-day TV show, *7th Heaven*. The preacher on the show has about seven kids, and most of his time is spent ministering to his family. I often laugh and say, "The guy never does anything for the church." A good chaplain is a lot of things: social worker, poor man's psychiatrist, priest, rabbi—whatever meets the need at the time.

I arrived with a rucksack and a flight bag with my belongings. I even had a supply of medical stuff my doc buddy had sent with me. Useless, I soon discovered, but when you're coming to Nam, who knows what you might need. I muscled the stuff over to the tent. Inside were two GIs, who looked up. Both jumped to their feet as though I'd caught them doing something. "Oh, sorry, Chaplain, we've been using the tent since you weren't around."

"No sweat," I said. We had a long look at each other. Then before I knew it, they were gone. I still was not very comfortable with my role as an officer and being part of the system, yet my sole purpose was to serve the soldiers. As mentioned before, the chaplaincy is actually older than the country itself. George Washington had his own chaplain. Having seen the movie *Patriot*, I always think that maybe that depiction of the chaplain is a good one. He leaves his flock and goes off to war. I didn't know how to be a chaplain at war so it was OJT (on-the-job training) for me.

At that point in my brief military experience, I had been in the Army about a year and was as green as grass. A captain came over and said, "Welcome. I'll show you around." He was the signal officer, and this was an act of kindness on his part. I felt lost at the moment. Fortunately, in days to come, I'd have the chance to repay him for his kindness. The poor guy always seemed to have a sign on his back that said, "Kick me" or "Blame me for it."

We went to the TOC (tactical operations center); it was a long building and you went down into it. There were field desks everywhere, commo (communications) equipment, and it looked like I imagined a war room should. Some chaplains seemed to know all that stuff, like who the S1 (personnel) is, what the adjutant did. How things operate.

Most of the time, I didn't have a clue but had the innate capacity to understand my role and what "showtime" meant—in other words, doing my job.

A tall lieutenant colonel appeared, looked me over, and didn't slow down. He was important, I guess. What I remember was the heat and the constant noise coming from somewhere, probably artillery fire; little booms.

I have some crazy memories of Mongoose. Since nobody told me what I was supposed to do or not do, I sat around for a day or so, got the lay of the land, and talked to just about everybody who would talk to me. I sat down at the mess tent drinking coffee for a couple of mornings—no Starbucks in the Nam.

I got to know Louie, the mess sergeant. What a fascinating guy. Scowling, running the mess hall with a kind of gruffness that is not real but *is* real. A big belly; I don't think he understood the concept of being in shape Army style. He had about half a dozen minions who went back and forth. The food was good—not *M\*A\*S\*H*-type meals. (Remember that in the TV program *M\*A\*S\*H*, they always showed the mess tent in the worst light: the food is terrible and unappetizing, not to mention unappealing.) Although I'm sure GIs griped, Louie's mess hall was very good and there was plenty of food. He personally dressed up the tables; he could have had his own Army cooking show. He knew presentation. He sat down at the end of the table once and said to me, "Chaplain, what in the hell are you doing here?" He was entirely serious.

"Just hanging out."

"No," he scowled, "I don't mean, what are you doing in this mess hall? What are you doing in this hellhole called Vietnam?"

Good question, I thought. "Well, I guess the soldiers might need me."

He didn't say anything but stared at me for a minute or two and finally said, "OK, I'll buy that, and so here's the question. What are you doing here?" He shook his head with an "I don't get it" gesture, got up, and went back to the back of the tent where the cooking took place. I just sat there.

Of all the places at Mongoose, and there weren't many where I could hang out, this seemed the friendliest. It was located just off the artillery

*At war, there's no such thing as Sundays, but one of the things I tried to do was have as many services as I could on a Sunday. It gave soldiers the semblance of normalcy and also kept them slightly centered, I felt. And, in war, whenever given the opportunity, soldiers will go to services. Chaplains in Iraq tell me they are finding this true also.*

section and belonged to the artillery battery I supported. There were so many things to learn. I didn't know what I needed to know. Does that make any sense? I thought for a moment maybe that was what Louie meant—What *am* I doing here? Not so much the question of why am I here in Vietnam, but *What am I doing here at Mongoose, in Vietnam, at war? What is my place?* Good questions.

*Forgetting what lies behind*
*and pressing forward to what lies ahead,*
*I press on toward the goal . . .*

PHILIPPIANS 3:13-14

# At War and Unwanted—
# Says Who?

I was still lost in thought when I was told the commander wanted to see me. I followed a troop down to the TOC. We went to the end of the bunker and stood outside a curtain where the CO (commanding officer) lived. The GI stuck his head inside and then motioned me in.

"Chaplain, have a seat."

I sat.

"You know, I'm pretty busy here, and to be honest, I never understand the chaplain's place in combat. I think you'd be better off back at Sally and maybe be ready to see our soldiers at the aid station. I don't want you out here because we don't have time to look after you. The troops are too busy to be concerned with anything but their jobs."

He acted like he wanted to say something else but stood up in a dismissive gesture and then simply went out. I was too dumb to realize I was being dismissed and followed him through a maze of radios and people. *What was wrong with me? I didn't need anybody looking after me. Why didn't I tell him, "Colonel, I'm Special Forces trained. Do you think that is nothing?"*

Being marginalized is a situation that confronts military chaplains all the time. By and large, we seem to be the only ones who realize our importance—at least it often seems that way. We are more likely than not to be marginalized because those in command don't see what we do as essential or important. Most chaplains never admit that this is happening, which makes it harder to deal with. Because we're in denial, we don't confront the system enough or make ourselves known. Unfortunately, many chaplains simply go along cooperating and graduating. They don't rock the boat, and most get promoted and climb the ladder. On occasion, one might even make chief of chaplains—by following a plan of "Don't make waves."

I knew many chaplains who were not content to let their roles be less than they should be. At this time in my military existence, I was more interested in how to serve while at war. I was in Vietnam to do a job. I didn't know exactly what it was, but I wanted to get on with it.

• • •

I figured I needed to gather up my stuff and check with somebody about getting a ride back to Sally. I didn't know enough to know what I should be doing at war anyway. I felt resigned to leaving.

Suddenly the air was still; it didn't even seem to be there. Someone was shouting *Incoming, Incoming.* People were running everywhere. I got behind sandbags with other soldiers. And then suddenly, almost right behind us, artillery began firing, answering the mortars that had been fired at us from a local village. It all lasted about five minutes, and then there was running, shouting, and firing.

A couple of GIs in the supply section got hit and someone called in a medevac. I walked over to the supply tent and one guy was sitting in a chair with blood all over him. Looked like he was hit in the shoulder. Another, a few feet away, was on the ground. I could feel my feet moving and my mouth uttering something.

"I'm the chaplain. God bless you," I said as I reached down and touched each of them. Both smiled slightly. I didn't have a clue what I was doing. Maybe the colonel was right: this wasn't the place for me. Later on, I saw both of the wounded GIs at the aid station, and they commented on how surprised they were to see me. I felt an unusual rapport with them. It felt good.

I had been up-country about a week and this was war. The next morning, the S1 sergeant saw me at breakfast and said that the CO had told him to get me a ride back to Sally. "So you're going back to hang out at Sally?"

"I guess so."

"You can join the S1 (he was talking about his lieutenant). You couldn't get him away from Sally with a keg of dynamite. He's counting his days—scared shitless," the sergeant said in a deep southern drawl as he grinned.

I sat there staring into space until a fairly rotund sergeant asked me if I wanted another cup of coffee. I looked at him getting it for me and thought that he was well on his way to replacing Louie, who suddenly appeared. Louie took the cup from him, passed it to me, and sat down.

"Chaplain, figured out yet why you're here?"

I hesitated a moment. "No, not really. The CO says for me to go back to Sally and maybe be available for guys when they get wounded."

"That m—f— doesn't know his ass from a hole in the ground. You need to be with the troops. They need you out in the field, not sitting around waiting for them to be killed."

I countered his comments with "But the commander said . . ." Before I could finish, he said, "Fuck the commander! Get your ass out in the field where those kids need you, or this is the last coffee you're getting from me." He smiled as he walked back to his inner sanctum.

That was a defining moment of my ministry in Vietnam. For some reason, Louie's statement sank into my psyche, and I realized he was right. I *didn't* come to Vietnam to sit around and wait for the war to come to me. I was a minister, my life was dedicated to service, and I wanted to be where I could do the most good. That was why I was in the Army.

Chaplains operated differently in Vietnam, and I don't criticize any of them for their approach to ministry if it was honest. In fact, I didn't, at this stage, even know how any of them *did* ministry. Some senior chaplains argued that being in the field with the troops was not the best place for a chaplain. They felt that if it did any good, it was slight at best.

I discovered later that some senior commanders cringed at the idea of a combat chaplain. If he were killed, what effect would it have on morale? I came to believe that many overestimated how hard it would be on the troops anyway. To be honest, I didn't have any views at this stage. But I did know this: I had not made all those sacrifices and done all those stupid things in training back at Bragg and Benning to be sitting around reading paperbacks.

*Saturday at 0630 Chaplain "A" conducted a prayer breakfast for the 54th Engineer Battalion. I led the music. The place was packed . . . Sunday was another blessing. Our guitar praise chorus continues to grow. We have almost twenty people in it now. We lost some soldiers when the CH-47 [helicopter] got shot down . . . This whole week was taken up with memorial services. We lost an engineer in a mine strike. We had a UH-60 [type of helicopter] go down. It has not been a good week.*

A CHAPLAIN IN IRAQ

*I offer neither pay nor quarters, nor food;*
*I offer only hunger, thirst, forced marches,*
*battles and death. Let him who loves his*
*country with his heart, follow me.*

GARIBALDI, ROME, 1849

# The Troops Are Waiting

What to do? I had been told to leave but knew I should stay. A helicopter was landing, and a lieutenant and three troops were heading toward it. To this day, I don't know what made me do it, but I hopped on that chopper, not having a clue where it was going but thinking it was heading for one of the companies. Sure enough, we landed in about five minutes. They all scurried off and I followed them.

With a burst of bravado that I didn't feel, I said, "Where's the CO?" A gaunt-looking GI stared at me and suddenly came to life. "Chaplain, wow, you're out here to visit us!" I suddenly felt like Santa Claus. He led me back to a clump of men sitting in the midst of three or four scraggly trees. He kept saying to GIs he was passing,

"It's the chaplain, it's the chaplain." Several jumped up, smiling and shouting, "Chaplain, chaplain." A couple reached out and touched me. I was almost overwhelmed. They were like bobbing dolls, up and down. Suddenly, I was eyeball to eyeball with a slight, handsome captain a few years younger than I was. "Damn, Chaplain, what a pleasant surprise. I'm John [not his real name]." Thus began an enormous friendship. He was so happy to see me and briefed me on everything they were doing. I felt important and thought, *This is it.*

He said, "You tell me what you want to do—have religious services, or what? Can you stay a few days?" What he didn't realize was that I could stay lots of days.

Being there was like an orientation to summer camp. Sure, I had been through Special Forces training and a few other things, but this was the real stuff. I was out with infantry soldiers, i. e., grunts, and we were at war. I was excited, scared, and trying to figure it all out. We walked, we took fire, we returned fire, we called in fire. We laid down covering fire. I was loving it.

Being a combat chaplain was not what I expected. First of all, the hard-to-believe acceptance of the troops, their utter willingness to share themselves, their tremendous desire to have me with them. Suddenly, I felt useful, less marginalized. During times when nothing was happening, they wanted to talk: talk about themselves, their families, their wives, their lives, and their spiritual condition. There was something very pure about a young soldier and his daily facing of death. To my fellow chaplains' consternation,

I became whatever a soldier needed me to become. If he needed a priest, which was often, I became one.

I can't tell you the number of confessions I heard. I didn't even know what a confession was in the Catholic sense. But many a GI would say, "Father, would you hear my confession?" No amount of trying to explain that I was not a "Father" made any difference. Time after time I would say to a kid, "I'm not a priest." He would say, "No sweat—will you do it?" Like he didn't hear me. A priest joined us in the field on occasion, but for the most part they were simply not available. We had many able and brave Catholic priests in Vietnam—they simply couldn't cover all the ground they needed to. Anyway, I believed that all men are priests. Didn't my church believe in the priesthood of the individual believer anyway? Absolutely—this is war!

# no Tibetan Louie

Coming back to Mongoose from the field, I felt a certain amount of elation. I had been tested in combat and had met the test. I hadn't done anything, but I was there. And although I was assured that getting fired on was routine, some situations were worse than others. A firefight wasn't always a knock-down drag-out battle, but you knew that if you were a combat soldier, they were coming—not *if* but *when*. When you're "in combat," you're always ready and always expecting the next fight.

I needed to report to Louie. I felt like a high school kid who had done what his dad told him and it worked out. Louie was my special friend. He was an alcoholic, and even in the early morning hours you could smell the booze slightly. But it surely didn't hurt his chow. He put out some great eats. Imagine lobster for the troops.

I did learn later that Louie was not above dealing in the black market. Lots of people like him probably did. They knew how to make a buck. Louie had things he could trade, which was the key to being a player. Also, he had a honey on the side, or so the troops said. He had met her in Saigon where he'd gone on a bender or two early on. He'd been to Vietnam in '64 and '65—the good old days, as he called them.

He'd joined the 2$^d$ Brigade right before Christmas, and because he had been to Vietnam before, he knew the lay of the land. Surprisingly, he didn't try to land one of the cushy jobs down south like he'd had before. I think it had to do with him trying to police himself—stay more structured—but unfortunately, it didn't seem to work.

I had lots of experiences with Louie–enough to fill a book! One came with Typhoon Bess. It was raining slightly and the wind had picked up as I walked toward the mess tent. A typhoon was something I'd never seen. In North Carolina, during high school, we had a hurricane or two. Hurricane Hazel did some damage in my little town, but she was nowhere near as severe as a typhoon. So it was raining, and all of a sudden, the water was waist deep. I remember watching it rise, amazed. A package floated by and I reached out and grabbed it. It was a long box and obviously had been a present sent from the States. Thinking maybe I could return it, I flipped open the top to see what it was. Inside were a pair of women's black panties and a bra. A note on top read, "From a loving wife to the man I love." *God bless America!*

We had to evacuate to the beach. Mongoose was inland about five miles. My little tent ended up being on the highest ground around and was taken over by the command group. This was pretty prophetic and kind of funny in a way since the commander had tried to expel me. We were miserable. Everything was wet and we were cold.

I wandered down toward where I thought some coffee might be. One of Louie's cooks came out and said, "Chaplain, Louie has the DTs and is shaking so bad—a chill or something. I think he's going to die. He really needs some help."

I knew a little about alcoholism as I'd done an internship at Dorothea Dix Hospital in North Carolina—known to all North Carolinians as Dix Hill—a premier spot for treating alcoholism. Talk about an education. I loaned the alcoholics money and believed their lies, but I learned. Louie was not going to die, but alcoholism is very difficult to deal with, and eventually it would get him in trouble if the commander found out.

In Vietnam, expediency was the rule. If someone did their job—or didn't do their job but also didn't cause problems—they could skate by with almost anything. Louie did his job—or had been doing it—but now he was incapable of doing it.

The rescuer came out in me. I talked to the doc to see if there was anything he could do. No, he didn't have the medicine. I knew the formula. Ordinarily, the black market would have had whisky, but in this case the typhoon had suspended operations. I caught a ride up to the MacV

(Military Assistance Command, Vietnam) compound in Hue. The doc told me that if anybody had any booze, they would. Luckily, the first person I saw was a guy I'd met at Bien Hoa when I first came in country. He gave me a couple of fifths of Jack Daniels and I got it to Louie.

Is this the role of the chaplain? Probably not. But Vietnam meant that the normal and orthodox were often thrown out the window. In some ways, a chaplain's unorthodox ministry is a metaphor for Vietnam. A weird war, sorry to the max, and all the rules go out the door.

I did have loyalty toward Louie. He looked after soldiers in the only way he could. He fed them and made sure that the food he sent to the field was just as good as that served to those in the rear. Occasionally he went out to the field and served it. The troops loved him. He'd often don whites and one of those big chef hats. He knew style—I'm not making him better than he was.

He was also generous to a fault. When I was going on R and R, he bought me a little Canon camera and said to take some pictures. He was not above lending GIs money to go home or on R and R with the realization that he'd never see the money again.

Just before I left Nam, I heard that Louie had walked into the back propeller of a helicopter and it cut his head off. When someone told me about it, I couldn't believe it. *No way!* I grieved for him and second-guessed myself. I think what happened emotionally is that his life had gone to hell to such a degree that he intentionally killed himself. And he'd been in Vietnam too long. I still remember that scene from *Apocalypse Now* where Colonel Kurtz, who has gone mad, is talking to Captain Willard. Kurtz is fat (Marlon Brando) and the lighting is dark. He dips his hand into a basin of water, scoops up the water and dumps it over his bald head. In that scene he reminds me of Louie.

I think that Louie, along with Colonel Kurtz, had Vietnam in his soul and it destroyed him. Louie had gotten fatter, drinking and eating excessively, and with each successive commander he was hassled a little more. He said he just wanted to go home, but things were not good on that front either. He had four kids: two older boys by his first wife, who, he said, was constantly hounding him for money and had gotten involved with one of their neighbors. His present wife was Korean, and they had two little boys whom he adored.

Maybe his wife was messing around. It was natural, he said. "I didn't meet her on a date. In Korea, these were business/working girls. Translate that as prostitute." Louie was drunk, but he insisted on telling me, "While you're in Korea, they look after all your needs. They trap you, you take them back home as your wife. They don't know anything but what they do. Maybe, I'm telling you." No amount of assuaging could convince him otherwise.

He had actually gone home on leave to straighten things out. I never found out what happened, but he came back early. He was in a major funk, drinking a quart of whisky a day, smoking pot, and most of the time doing nothing. It affected his work. I talked to him constantly to no avail. It was sad for me, as I was losing a friend, and I often thought back to our first encounter that set the stage for my ministry. *Get yourself out in the field where the troops need you!*

The one other person who missed Louie as much as I did was White Elephant, one of our *hoi chanhs*. (These were former VC who, for various reasons, switched sides). We were always a little suspicious of *hoi chanhs*, but White Elephant had proven his worth and the GIs loved and trusted him. Louie had looked after him. White Elephant cut a fancy swath around the campus, as Louie called the base. He wore a couple of Roy Rogers cap pistols that somebody's mother had sent from the States. He had seen a Roy Rogers western and had adopted Roy's persona. He wore leather cowboy boots and stuffed his jungle fatigue trousers in them. With his cap guns tied securely to his legs like an Old West gunslinger, he was ready for a quick draw, which he was always practicing.

Talking to White Elephant was a respite from war. He learned some GI language but mostly he knew English words, and he strung them together in gosh-awful sentences. I had to talk to him constantly about cursing. He spoke pidgin English, and calling it English is generous. The GIs loved him and pretended they knew exactly what he was saying when they didn't understand a word.

White Elephant always came to worship services and sat in the front row. If we were in the field, he sat right beside the makeshift altar, never taking his eyes off me. He acted like he understood every word. Louie told me that he had taught White Elephant to say "Amen" and that I should let him have the final Amen in a service sometime. The idea was that I would pray the benediction and then point at him or pause for a minute and he could say the final amen. Louie had White Elephant prove his "Amen" prowess a couple of times for me and I pronounced him ready.

As a symbolic gesture, I decided that White Elephant's first public Amen would be at Louie's memorial service— it would be his final tribute to Louie. When we came to the benediction, I paused and glanced at White Elephant and nodded. He jumped to his feet and came out with a loud *HooAhhhhhhhhhhhhhhh, airborne!* Louie had to be laughing.

*For we know that if the earthly tent*
*we live in is destroyed,*
*we have a building from God,*
*a house not made with hands,*
*eternal in the heavens.*

II CORINTHIANS 5:1

*Georges Clemenceau is reputed to have said that war was too important to be left to soldiers. Nobody seems to have come forward with the obvious corollary, which is that peace is too precious to be left to politicians.*

MARSHAL ANDREWS IN THE FOREWORD TO THE BOOK *STREET WITHOUT JOY* BY BERNARD B. FALL

# Care of the Soldier Trumps the Mission

Young company commanders in Vietnam were my heroes. I was probably five years older than most of them. They seemed to have a maturity—a sort of leadership quality that put their lives on hold and made them superhuman. To me, they were all terrific. I don't remember much about John's background, for instance. We became fast friends. When I was not out with his company as often as I could be, he was on the horn wanting to know where I was.

Most company commanders served at least six months as line company commanders. This was tough beyond description. They were the decision makers. I often thought that these young men, if they made it through the war, could do literally anything. Combat not only prepared but steeled these men for future pressure, decisions, and life. It also gave them a sense of perspective. Nothing they would face in the future would be remotely like the life and death decisions they had to make in combat. They were carrying out the command's directives, but they put their own footprint on them. Most of the young commanders were absolutely the best.

Of course, they were different from each other as all people are different. Some were more cautious; others more daring. Occasionally one might be over the top. To a person, however, they maintained a fierce tenacity about the lives of their soldiers. When their troops died, a little of them died, too.

When I was at Command and General Staff College at Leavenworth, Kansas, I still had Vietnam in my psyche, and I decided to write a fictional account of my experiences. John served as my lead character. It was not hard to make him bigger than life. What I liked about him and learned quickly was that he definitely listened to the beat of a different drummer. First, he had figured out that Vietnam was a sorry war—a war that was, in a sense, unwinnable. I don't know why he felt that way and don't remember talking about it. Action was always a little too heavy and when you're getting shot at, philosophy takes a back seat. But, he had it figured out and early on decided that his "care of the troops" would trump the "mission."

He was one cool dude. The command would call him from the TOC and say, "This is Bold Eagle" (or Racing Falcon or whatever the battalion commander's call sign was) and tell him to move to certain map coordinates. Most of the time, John took out his map, looked at the route, and checked to see what the situation was and what the likely potential action would be. He'd answer, "Roger." And then he'd do nothing. Some time later, he'd call in his position at where they thought he would be. He wouldn't take chances, because he knew war and calculated which position would be most likely to keep his soldiers out of contact. He didn't do this all the time, but he outsmarted the command based on his care of his troops. It was his goal never to put them in jeopardy—no easy task, but I don't remember a time when he was wrong.

I sometimes thought about whether his approach was good but learned quickly not to second guess him. When you're out there in action, in constant crisis, in life-and-death situations, the rules go out the door.

*For those who fight for it, freedom has a*
*flavor the protected will never know.*

FOUND ON A C-RATION BOX
AT THE BATTLE OF KHE SANH, 1968

# I Spent a Year in Vietnam One Night

During my time in Nam, I became a good soldier, almost too good in a sense. I could read maps, direct artillery if need be—almost anything. I would go out on *tigers* (the code name for a patrol) with the troops, taking useless and needless chances.

I carried a weapon. Why? To me, it was practical. For the first couple of months, I didn't. Most chaplains didn't. It really was not our job. But, I noticed the troops seem to be uncomfortable: they still had the idea that I had to be protected. When I began carrying a weapon, they were less concerned because I was not someone they had to look after. In a sense, I was one of them. I never had a soldier ask me why I had a weapon.

The weapon and the soldiering aspect of the Nam experience gave me little pause throughout my post-Vietnam time in the Army. The weapon probably would have gone unmentioned except for a single incident. In some ways, it began innocently and routinely. I was at the fire support base one day eluding the brass when our battalion commander spied me. We had become good buddies. By this time, I'd been in Vietnam about eight months.

We were at Sandy, a different fire support base from where I'd started. It was made in a five-point shape and from the air it looked like a star. We had a new recon platoon leader going out for the first time. He was obviously green as grass and also scared. Now, did he tell anybody he was scared? I doubt it. But I could tell—it's a sixth sense you get after you've been in Nam for a while. You sense when things are just not right—not kosher. *Why not go out with him,* the commander hinted. *Give him a little confidence.*

*No sweat,* I thought. I walked down to where the platoon was waiting. Several of the guys were getting ready, looking weary, and, of course, they possessed the thousand-yard stare. It's that vacant look that says you've been in Nam too long and had too many experiences. It's a combination of boredom, tedium, fear of the worst, and dread of what's coming that makes a person just block everything out.

I walked around, good-naturedly hassled a few guys, leaned back against some sandbags, and started writing a letter. I always wrote one page a day—it's kind of a positive addiction of mine.

We saddled up and walked past the artillery out to the perimeter. I waved to a couple of artillery guys leaning on one of their pieces—again the thousand-yard stare. They'd watched the same procession hundreds of times and were glad they were in the artillery. Being a *redleg* (in the artillery) was not a day at the beach either, but overall it was better than being a good old ground-pounder. If they got killed, it would be the VC coming after them, throwing in some mortars and overrunning the perimeter, but this was different from being a grunt. A grunt was going to die. He was destined to it. He was cannon fodder.

We all sat and stared waiting for the choppers. It was March and it was hot. We'd just come through the monsoon, an incredibly cold time. Most who don't know Vietnam think it's a hot place, but during a couple of months, it can freeze your behind off. And when it rains, you get colder. But today it was hot.

I wondered what the lieutenant was thinking. He was a nice-looking kid in his early twenties. He probably couldn't get his macho out of the way. Why did the chaplain have to go with him? I didn't know what the CO had told him, so I decided to lighten the machismo some. "Lieutenant, thanks for letting me ride along with you. I'm going to join up with B Company and they're close to you. So I'm tired of sitting around. The worst thing over here, if you haven't figured it out yet, is the boredom. You'll never get down to a two-digit midget [a magic number that indicates that you're closer to going home] if you don't keep moving." I smiled. He was quiet and nodded.

He probably didn't know what to make of me. Military training is pretty slack in how line officers should interact with chaplains, lawyers, and doctors. There's definitely no manual for how they all work together in war, especially one like Vietnam.

For the Nam soldier, there were incredible oscillations of spirit. From a sort of nervous excitement to an overwhelming sense of dread. I couldn't tell which the lieutenant was feeling. I don't think he bought what I'd said about my presence anyway. In a crazy way which is part of Nam, he didn't care and I didn't care.

He was probably a West Point graduate. He'd been in the Army since November and now it was March. It fit: graduated from West Point, got married, and had a nice honeymoon. Next went off to Officer Basic at Benning. Maybe to ranger and airborne school and then Nam. I felt sorry for him. These were the times that I was most angry about Vietnam.

This young guy had his whole life ahead of him, and here he was a step away from dying. Well, some say, he had gone to a military school and should have known what he was getting into. I never believed that! None of these kids went to West Point or the Citadel or ROTC thinking that one day they're going to be in Vietnam or at war or dead. They didn't think in those terms. They were young and invincible.

They were going to college. Well, West Point is hardly college. In a sense, it is: both a college where academia is king and a leadership course for soldiers. But right then, all that existed for them was Vietnam. *I want to go to Vietnam, I want to kill some Vietcong.*

I'd never seen a bad West Point Officer, not just in Nam but throughout my military career. I mean bad in the sense of someone not pointed in the right direction. Most of the young officers in Nam were a mixed bag. Most were good but some might be better employed other places than at war. The only way to even ponder such a thing is retrospectively.

Most officers were commissioned through college ROTC, OCS (officer candidacy school) and, of course, West Point. Rarely did I see a man who had a "direct commission," or, as it was popularly called, a *battlefield commission*. We did have a company commander who had received a battlefield commission in our unit when I first came. He was older and had come up through the ranks. As the story goes, he was overcautious, which our brigade commander, who later became a general, didn't appreciate, so he fired the company commander.

I saw some ROTC guys who obviously did not have a military calling and some from OCS who should not have been commissioned at all. Someone like William Calley (the lieutenant of My Lai fame who lead the slaughter of unarmed villagers) probably should never have been put in a situation like Vietnam. You can think what you want about My Lai—it's awful and tragic any way you look at it because of bad decisions, poor judgment, and a thousand and one other things. But, in a situation like war, where your men are being killed daily, you're in a constant state of anxiety; you don't know who the enemy is, and bad things happen. Judgment can become impaired. Some days it's pretty clear what's right and wrong, but about a guy like Calley, who maybe didn't have much emotional sophistication and was not overly smart, I would never be too judgmental.

At some time, he may have seen his men blown up by a female VC with a grenade hidden in her apron. Or he may have witnessed a water buffalo boy scoping out his position so he could relay it to the VC, who would attack them with mortars.

At some time during his sojourn in Vietnam, an officer would be thrown into a chaotic, confusing situation. Maybe this is not what happened with Lieutenant Calley, but he certainly was ill-prepared and ill-equipped. Understanding, tempered with mercy, is not a bad thing. A commander once told me that everybody in Vietnam is in somebody's army.

*It is one of life's laws
that as soon as one door closes,
another opens.
But the tragedy is that we look
at the closed door
and disregard the open one.*

ANDRÉ GIDE

# Get Ready.
# Sound Off for Equipment
# Check—Stand in the Door

In Vietnam, things often start out routinely. Three slicks (choppers/helicopters) suddenly appeared in the distance. The RTO (radio telephone operator) said, "Here they come." We boarded. I had been on hundreds of combat assaults, or so it seemed. It was one of the tactics of the Vietnam war. Surprise the enemy: swoop in with the helicopters loaded with troops. It sounded good, but I was never sure it worked all that well. In this case, today, things had been quiet in this AO (area of operations) for some time and nobody expected anything to happen, not the CO, not me, surely not the lieutenant.

I was always a little apprehensive. The lieutenant got on the first chopper. I was on the last. There seemed to be about thirty guys on board. I was never good at knowing how many were in a platoon, a company, whatever. What was there was there. We were choppering out to the edge of a small ville, where we were to sweep through the unoccupied village. We were in a free-fire zone. Anybody who was not us was the enemy. Once on the ground, we were to proceed toward the ocean and link up with B Company. I wasn't sure I had it all just right, since it didn't matter to me one way or another. *Just do it!*

One of the things I never got involved in was command business. I never forgot that I was a chaplain. It may not have looked like it at times, because I had the trappings of a combat soldier—the rucksack, the knife, the weapon—but I *was* the chaplain—the preacher in uniform, the spiritual leader. In a pinch, I would serve the soldier in whatever way he needed, at least in my own limited way. On this day, I was serving him by being a soldier, one who was with him.

Improvising was one of my best skills. For instance, I discovered that when a soldier was killed (and that was often—for a period of months, five to ten of our men were killed every day), his fellow troopers were not only unnerved but went into a type of shock—they didn't want to just go on with what they were doing. I devised a short ceremony—a sacrament, I called it. I'd kneel before the fallen soldier, bow my head, make the sign of the cross, and then touch the body with my hand or a cross or stole (a stole is like a scarf, usually with a cross embroidered on it) if it were handy. I was a long way from those days at the ARP (Associate Reform Presbyterian) Seminary when my good buddy talked me into thinking about the chaplaincy.

*Grant us wisdom from Thy mind,*
*Courage from Thine heart*
*and protection by Thine hand.*
*It is for Thee that we do battle,*
*and to Thee belongs the victor's crown.*
*For Thine is the kingdom and the power*
*and the glory forever.*

GREEN BERET PRAYER,
FROM THE SPECIAL FORCES CHAPEL,
FORT BRAGG, NORTH CAROLINA

*God, give us men!*
*A time like this demands strong minds,*
*great hearts, true faith and ready hands . . .*

JOSIAH HOLLAND

# Waiting on the Green Light—GO!

We landed: one, two, three. Efficient. Suddenly, all hell broke loose. Firing was coming from everywhere. I did what soldiers always do when they come under fire— laid down some fire at something. It was already getting dark. Suddenly, it was eerily quiet, and I scrambled back behind a cemetery mound. The Vietnamese burial grounds were usually circular, and the gravesites were mounds of varying heights. I had heard that they buried their dead sitting up. I wasn't sure of all my surroundings, as when you take fire, there is an out-of-this-world feeling. You're simply carried to another place, running on adrenalin. I couldn't hear anything. There was sporadic fire. I didn't know where anybody was. Out in front of me, I could see some troopers hugging the ground behind the mounds. One was dead, I was pretty sure, as he was so still and

I thought I saw blood oozing and forming a big round patch. I started crawling and saw another soldier who had been hit and looked gone. Where was the RTO? I needed that radio! The RTO was catatonic. I said, "What happened?"

He said nothing. I told him to call the platoon leader. Nothing. I heard sporadic fire again. A burst of AK-47 rounds crackled over my head. I could see the muzzle flashes. Somewhere there was a 30-caliber machine gun sounding off. It definitely wasn't ours. They were firing mortars as well. Later on, somebody told me they were 82s—*that's great to know!*

"Switch to the operations net at Battalion," I said as I shook him, which seemed to wake him up. He fumbled in his pocket and got out his radio frequency pad. I took the radio. "This is Preacher Man"—I didn't even remember if that was my call sign, but I knew they'd recognize my voice. "We don't know what happened, but we're taking heavy fire, can't raise six, over." More hell broke loose. Rounds were whipping past and dirt was kicking up. It was one of those adrenalin-pumping, gushing moments. I was scared senseless and remember telling myself to get a grip.

I know it sounds a little John Wayne, but suddenly the thought popped into my mind that we were about to be overrun by the enemy. I pulled a dead trooper toward me and prepared myself to get his weapon and ammo bandoleer. Then I started looking around for somebody with a sixty (M60 machine gun). We were going to have to put up a fight. Suddenly, one of our Cobra gunships was overhead. Then there were two, opening up on the enemy—Gatling–gun-style with a few rockets thrown in for good measure. I hoped B Company was closing in. *Thank you, Lord!* The lieutenant and most of those on the first bird were killed, I figured. The gunship left.

In Nam, we always expected the unexpected, and this was it. For weeks, everything had been quiet in this area—no activity. We heard rumors later that an entire battalion of NVA (North Vietnamese Army) soldiers had been dug in underground. For weeks, we'd heard about the NVA—hard cases, as they were known. The VC would hit you and run, but the NVA would keep coming at you and at you. We surprised them and were lucky that any of us survived. They probably went back underground when the Cobras showed up. The NVA or VC had tunnels that were like cities—all they had to do was scurry back down like rats. We'd never find them.

I didn't know what to do. Any minute, in my mind's eye, more gunships or B Company could come to our rescue. All was quiet—even the radio. By now it was dark. I hate the dark; everything bad happens at night.

I had to find out how many of us were alive. I tried to calculate how many men we had to begin with. A recon platoon is supposed to have 40 to 60 men. I asked the RTO, who was still half in shock, to see if he could reach any of the squads. I crawled up to the mound where one of the troopers had been hit. He was dead. I whispered to another I could barely see. The RTO low-crawled up beside me. He told me he thought there were about eight guys in front of us. I took the radio and said, "Spread out.

Establish a killing zone." (A killing zone is an area in front of you, between you and other troops, coming to a point like a cone, that gives you the best chance of getting someone who's moving toward you). Once you set it up, you have to wait; the idea is to catch them between you and the other troops. If they were in front of us, which it appeared they were, we needed simply to establish our own limited perimeter. Then we'd have the back and sides covered, and they'd at least have to come and get us. I didn't have a clue where the starlight scope was or even if we had one. This was an impossible mess!

The radio crackled: "Give us a sitrep (situation report), over."

"We have several kilos and many whiskies," I said.

The CO said, "We're working on extraction. Sit tight." Later on, I discovered he was talking to Brigade. They were deciding what to do. He came back on and said, "We're going to light up the area. Keep your heads down. We can't get you extracted until first light. Over"

"First light?"

"Roger." *This was going to be a long night.*

## How Shall We Die?

This is why I love soldiers. One of my buddies of over 30 years sent me this e-mail when I asked him about what he remembered from that night.

*I tell you, that night was the closest to a mutiny that I ever saw in Vietnam. I was on the radio when you came on. It got deathly quiet. We were scrambling. The captain told the colonel that we had to do something. They checked the coordinates. When it looked like you were going to be out there all night, I was sick. I told a few people. The word spread. Suddenly, we had a platoon of guys with weapons ready to combat assault into the AO. The colonel was incredulous, but I told him, "We're going."*

*"I'm ordering you to stay put."*

*I cursed him. The captain calmed us, gathered us all in the colonel's briefing room, and explained what was going on—they were keeping flares on you all night, gunships were ready, and if there was any contact, they were on the way. At first light, you and the men would be picked up. It calmed us, but several of the guys weren't convinced.*

*"It is going to be hell to pay," one of the men told the captain, "if anything happens to the chaplain. I'm going to kill the son of a bitch [meaning the colonel]."*

*I think that it is very fortunate that many of us trusted the captain because he'd been my CO in C Company. None of us slept a bit that night. Man, I'm telling you, we were ready.*

The night passed and the sky stayed lit up like daylight. I didn't sleep at all, and thought about many things: the obvious ones like Jackie and Meg, but I felt more sad than scared in a sense. How is it that some men die and some live? Most of us do the sorts of things that we were told would help our chances, and yet, men still died: two guys were side by side, and one lived and one died. *I hate war.*

The next morning, when it got light, it was like an armada, all of C Company combat-assaulted in and B Company was facing us, and then the dustoffs started coming. The S3 (operations officer) had taken over, and I boarded one of the medevacs. Several GIs had been killed or wounded, including the new, young lieutenant. I'd never even gotten to know him.

Am I remembering it worse than it was? Now looking back, I think not—it was even worse than I've described. A reporter had been at the TOC when I radioed in. Somebody had screamed out, "That's the chaplain," and everybody started scrambling. The reporter sniffed a story and wrote it up and I was forever branded as the "gun-totin' chaplain."

*You've gone ahead before us, to well-earned rest,*
*Having given to this life your very best.*
*There's a private place, Darling, where you'll never depart,*
*And there you're very much alive—It's a special corner of my heart.*
*You volunteered for combat, Leaving the children and me,*
*You went to help the battle to keep other people free.*
*I know, could we turn back the years, you would do it all again,*
*In your quiet gentle manner you died helping your fellow man.*
*You won't go down in history books or ever remain immortal.*
*But I know God said: "Well done, My son,"*
*when you entered Heaven's portal.*
*So in my own way, Darling, I've written this remembrance to you—*
*No one here can know how much I miss you—*
*But I somehow feel you do. I love you, Babbie*

BARBARA CONRAD WROTE THIS POEM
THE DAY SHE WAS NOTIFIED THAT HER HUSBAND
HAD BEEN KILLED IN VIETNAM

# The Good Die Young

When I look back at the lives lost in Vietnam, I want to curse and cry, and I always think, *What a senseless war.* My mantra for those we lost in Vietnam was given to me by another vet: "They may have died in vain, but they lived in honor." I want to call their names as my friends are very personal to me, but the thought of leaving someone out, not having permission, or hurting them or their families is too disturbing for me. I will never forget those fallen soldiers and our camaraderie, and they are forever a part of my psyche. I cannot remember a bad young commander. Because of who they were—their personalities—some stick out. What I didn't see among them was the sort of personal ambition to rise in rank or status at the expense of their troops that was all too evident at the higher levels.

Robby (not his real name) was the Delta Company commander. What made him stand out was his sense of humor and absolute bravado. First of all, his personal military history was not too shabby. He graduated as the "goat" at West Point. I didn't have a clue what that meant at the time, but he loved to talk about it. When cadets are in their final year and are last in the class or close to it, the challenge to be the goat heats up. Those in competition for goat status know exactly how many points are needed to pass or fail each quiz. When the semester ends, the victor is crowned as the last in the class. Goats are hailed by the student body and given great honor, as much or in some cases more than if they were at the top of the class. Robby was last, and he reveled in it.

I can tell you for a fact that his goat status was not reflected in his leadership. He was a terrific leader and the troops loved him. They respected him for his principles and his decisions. They'd follow him into hell. Robby was his own person.

Occasionally the military, then as now, makes stupid decisions in matters whose handling should be routine or common sense. One had to do with when a dignitary was coming to visit the field. The troops had to wear their complete uniform, with a shirt, not just a T-shirt. Thinking how stupid this was in the middle of the day when troops were trying to rest in 100-plus degree temperature, Robby invariably intentionally defied the edict and went shirtless to meet the general.

He was, in today's parlance, "bad." He made sure the general knew that he had to interrupt his routine for the briefing and also that the general was aware of his personal disdain for a stupid rule. Often commanders hovered in their helicopters over a battle or firefight. Most of the time there was no reason or benefit for this. At first Robby got furious about the practice; later he made fun of it: "Yeah, they're like a circus. You have the battalion commander in his Charlie Charlie (command and control) ship. Above him, you have the brigade commander looking for a medal, then above him, the CG, looking for another star. Assholes."

Most of the time he did his act for my benefit and not in front of the troops. He was too good an officer to show disrespect even for those he didn't think deserved it. He laughed and was animated, often looking to the sky and giving the one-finger salute. I laughed and loved it, because it showed a kind of belligerence aimed at an insane situation.

To Robby, the war was up close and personal. It was almost as though he was inviting someone to relieve him.

I think he would have hated to leave his soldiers, but then again, he was sick of the war and realized the futility of it. He was still in Vietnam when I left and later was killed. I heard that he extended in order to stay with his company, making him the longest-serving company commander in Vietnam. It sounds exactly like something he would do and was probably related to the challenge of being the goat at West Point. What a loss! He said to me with regularity, "Don't know what I'll do after Vietnam; it's too much in me. Don't think I'd be fit for anything else." I didn't get it then, I do now. *He may have died in vain but lived in honor.*

The tenure for company commanders usually was not long. I remember overall about a dozen men who were company commanders. A couple were older and had been enlisted guys—they either went to OCS or got battlefield commissions. They were good. What happened to many of them afterward was simply shameful—a product of incredible mismanagement at best or callousness at worst. It's hard for me to know how many of them were summarily sent out of the Army with nothing. It was called a RIF (reduction in force). The real term is firing. These guys had given their life's blood for their country. They were cannon fodder, and when they were used up, they were thrown out like yesterday's newspaper.

Much of the reason for this then and today has to do with politics, but increasingly, it has to do with the general public literally having no investment in the military. At this writing, only one member of Congress has a son or daughter in the military. Those making decisions to send kids off to war should have a personal investment in it—

they should be a part of it and not detached. Over the long haul, it is hard to know what it means. What I see today is that the president and members of Congress are paying someone else's children to fight America's battles; in effect, they're treating those children as mercenaries. It is absolutely immoral.

In Vietnam, we still had some semblance of the draft. The draft, I think, contributed to how veterans were treated after the war, probably psychologically more than officially. Because going to war was not the draftees' own choice, maybe a debt was owed them. Any who thought about it might have felt that draftees could have avoided the draft if they had had connections or were socially prominent. The view was that those who went to Vietnam were either stupid or simply unlucky. Otherwise they could have gotten out of going, as scores of other Americans did, many of whom have become prominent, like the former and the present commanders-in-chief.

Another pervasive view was that Vietnam warriors didn't believe in their cause or were there simply because of the draft. This is categorically not true. There were many in Nam who made the choice to serve when they could easily have gotten out of it. It was a pivotal event in the life of their generation and they wanted to be a part of it. They may not have articulated it then, but they certainly can now. For some, the explanation is not so complicated: they saw their duty and did it.

Company commanders were dedicated, and a successful command often assured them of future success. Over the years I've heard of scores of guys who served at the highest levels who were successful in Vietnam as young commanders. Many of them today are in public life, and in many ways it appears that their war experience served them well over all. I'm not sure this is universally true—there are as many stories as there are soldiers, and I know only a few. It's a case for the military draft or some kind of universal service.

*It is the endings
that often make the beginnings possible.*

FROM THE BOOK *TRANSITIONS*

# Shell-Shocked

They took fire. The platoon laid down fire. Where was the artillery? Sergeant Henry never failed to call it in. His rep was that he could have the artillery on a mortar muzzle flash a thousand meters away in something like milliseconds. The usual modus operandi for Sir Charles was to dump five or six rounds at your position, pick up his mortar tube, and run. With Sergeant Henry, he had to be careful.

It happened one day without warning. Platoon Sergeant Henry didn't respond. One of the platoon guys told the CO that Sergeant Henry couldn't seem to move. He was almost catatonic and was breaking out in a cold sweat—not a good thing in combat, especially a firefight. He'd get the shakes and then he'd say *I'll get over it*.

They carried him both literally and figuratively for a while, but then they couldn't. It came to a head with a firefight and all hell breaking loose—the momentary chaotic nightmare and the men waiting for Henry to call in artillery fire or at the very least limber up their own mortars—*Where was he?*—totally freaked out according to his RTO. He just shook and couldn't move.

Vietnam was populated with scores of heroes and other people who gave their all. Until that horrendous day, Sergeant Henry was the epitome of military leadership perfection—only one R and R (rest and relaxation) in four years and a leave home and now this. What do we do when a living legend—a hero—falters at war? *Send him to the chaplain.*

This was not the first time a chaplain had served as a repository for battle-fatigued leaders, but it seemed an unusual answer for a combat shell-shocked leader like Sergeant First Class Henry. Over the course of time, company commanders discovered that some of their best NCOs, especially platoon sergeants, reached a breaking point. They had to be removed from the field for the troops' good and for their own good. Where to send them to finish their few remaining months without ruining a faithful NCO's career was a heavy issue, not to mention protecting the lives of those under his command. The answer seemed to be the chaplain.

So Sergeant Henry came in to be with me. What a soldier! He was legendary. The troops trusted him like a god. He had single-handedly killed and brought havoc on scores of VC, and during the Tet offensive had been one of the first to fully understand what they were fighting and who they were fighting. No longer the black pajama-clad clandestine VC but the formidable NVA regulars. Therefore, Sergeant Henry set up training sessions in the field so his troops could learn how best to fight the NVA. According to him, fighting NVA soldiers was entirely different from fighting other types of enemy. They were better trained and tactically more superior, and when they hit, it would be in greater mass and with greater fury.

There were all kinds of rumors about the NVA—they had tanks, they had weapons never before seen, and even that they drank some sort of concoction that steeled them for battle—a type of getting high. Sergeant Henry had one view of all of that—BS.

Sergeant Henry, I later discovered, had a daughter with spina bifida. He really doted on her, and his wife had managed to keep her alive long past when she was expected to die. His staying in Vietnam was absolutely essential to her well-being as he saw it. Although the doctors and hospitals had been good, there were lots of expenses and it was the extra combat pay that kept the family from needlessly suffering.

Robby was his company commander and I remember him saying to me, "Chaplain, you've got to keep him with you for 30 days, then we'll get him home. But, if you don't, it will be a mess and jeopardize his career. He's too good and has sacrificed too much for us not to do all we can to save him." He smiled. *Yeah, I hear you.*

It was a good couple of months. Honestly, I cannot tell you how much I learned. How to be a better soldier. What it means to have what Sergeant Henry called "the feeling"—that sixth sense that tells you when you're going to get hit. How to instill confidence in soldiers and never let them know you're scared or that this is anything but a job.

Sergeant Henry was the one who set me straight on weapons. The S3 had insisted I take his Car 15. I loved that weapon. It was a shorter version of the M16 with a collapsible stock. What I liked about it was that to me it was pretty unobtrusive. I could hang it on my shoulder and kind of slide it to my back to make it unnoticeable. All the troops knew I had a weapon and nobody thought anything about it. But I was self-conscious. There were no Berzerkeley (Berkeley) philosophers and antiwar types sitting around wondering about the chaplain carrying a weapon.

I did have a plan, though. I still was very sensitive and I voiced it to Sergeant Henry. If I got into a situation and had to use my weapon, I didn't intend to. It was for show, to keep the troops from feeling they had to look after me. Sergeant Henry, in his professor-like way, all but said, "Chaplain, that is the dumbest thing I've ever heard." To him, the issue was not "if" I ever might use it but "when" I was going to have to.

"One of these days," he said, "there'll be no choice. In order to protect yourself—or more importantly, your soldiers—you'll have to use that great little weapon, and when you do, you want to make sure you're effective." He convinced me. The idea that something might happen and I'd be unprepared made me know that I had to let the master instruct me. Sergeant Henry cleaned the weapon, showed *me* how to clean it, showed me how to quickly unjam it if it jammed, which he said would invariably happen. "It's a great weapon! And you better not call it a gun." He'd laugh and say this over and over.

We went south a couple of times to SERTS (Screaming Eagle Replacement Training School) to practice firing. Finally, we had to go to where the Special Forces had a mini jump school run by the South Vietnamese. For a carton of Camels, the Vietnamese NCO let us use a building they'd set up as a practice range. "You ain't no sniper," Sergeant Henry would say. "You don't aim, you point and squeeze if you are shooting at an individual target. More likely, you'll be laying down fire, so you rake the weapon back and forth." He'd demonstrate. His philosophy was that it all happened fast. "This ain't no quick draw in Tombstone. Squeeze and fire, rake that weapon. Start off on semi (automatic) and then switch to full automatic in one motion." After firing thousands of rounds—another carton of Camels for the ammo—he finally said, "Chaplain, you 'bout qualified, but that's it." He laughed and shook his head.

The only time Sergeant Henry got miffed at me was when I was waiting for him at the firing range and a couple of Special Forces types were going to jump out of a helicopter and offered me an extra chute if I wanted to jump. I did. It was fun, but Henry was irritated. "You don't know these Green Beret wienies (an insulting term often used to describe Special Forces troops) or who packed the chute! Who's going to look after the soldiers?" He was mad.

Now that I look back on it, I don't have a clue as to how I was able to keep Sergeant Henry hidden. Luckily, I conjured up several bogus trips south, but while we were at Bien Hoa at Division Rear, we got hit with a ground attack including some sappers. Talk about an eye-opener. For some crazy reason, up until that time I had in my mind that all the action was up north. Wrong—in Vietnam everywhere was the war.

During the attack, Sergeant Henry was as cool as a cucumber. He manned a bunker and called in artillery several times. After that, it was easy to maneuver him into a job as security manager with the rear for the rest of his tour. Nobody questioned it, and they thought I was doing them a great favor.

Pretty dicey. For one thing, had we been questioned, no way would the higher-ups have let a combat NCO out of the field. It would have been the TOC (tactical operation center) or back at brigade or division headquarters at best for him.

Making the decisions on winning a sorry war was likely made by those whose interests were more parochial than anything else. Letting experienced military types, for whatever reason, out of the field was not part of the plan. And, the troops needed the best out there. But even the best, like SFC Henry, had to function, and if they couldn't, I had to do something to help them.

*You might as well laugh as cry.*

G. R. AUTRY, PHILOSOPHER, 1898–1960

# Mail Call

What do you do when you're not fighting? Well, if you're the chaplain, you talk, you visit with the troops, you listen, you be who you are. You tell stories. I heard some super ones: war stories, stories about the family, stories about Army life. Sometimes, it's the macho, man thing; stories get better with a beer or two. I loved to hear the troops talk about the Army—it was a constant love/hate relationship.

Our resident was a great storyteller. He had been in A Company, a long time RTO to the company commander, and had an unusual wartime savvy that often pulled me through. (Even after Nam we kept in touch, and he's the one who got me involved with vets over the long haul. He called me years after the war and said, "Let's go to the dedication of the Wall in DC." I really didn't want to do it, but he was insistent. I was the division chaplain in the 82$^{\text{d}}$ Airborne by then, and busy. But he would have none of it. He came down and the night before we left for the dedication, and we saw the first Rambo movie, *First Blood*.)

In Vietnam, there were many times when I simply didn't know what to do. I fought feelings of hopelessness, remorse, and simply wondering, *What am I doing here? This is crazy.* Often during those times our storyteller stepped up to the plate without even knowing it. He had the southern storyteller gene in him. It has been said that all southerners possess this gene, which enables them to make a story out of everything. He had a double portion. I doubt seriously if there was a better storyteller anywhere. I loved to listen to any war story, but especially his, and when things got tough and I had a few moments for reflection, I'd smile remembering a story or two of his.

Our unit had taken an unusual number of hits—we had a 70 percent casualty rate over a six-month period, the highest ever of any unit in Vietnam. Tensions were running high. We had just had a hassle with a sergeant major who was in charge of the mailroom.

He'd disappear all of a sudden, leaving a pile of mail that couldn't be distributed until he returned. Most of the time no one had a clue where he was. Probably gone south on some boondoggle or blackmarketing in the ville.

To say he was not respected is an understatement. Once I distributed the mail, which was totally illegal, because we couldn't find the guy. He went bananas. I would have gotten in a jam, but somebody told me that one of the troops told the sergeant major that if he said anything, one night a grenade might just find its way into his tent. I never heard anything else.

The sanctity of mail to soldiers in combat cannot be over estimated. It is the single greatest morale booster in war. It is the last remaining connection they have to their family, values, and roots. Today, soldiers have access to e-mail and faxes and other things, but then it was just the APO (Army post office), mostly run by soldiers whose motivation often left something to be desired. Knowing the sanctity of the mail and how the mail was handled makes me shudder.

*War is delightful (only) to those*
*who have not experienced it.*

DESIDERIUS ERASMUS

*God lives in the paddy preacher,*
*No doubt is there in me,*
*That the doggie reverend, a rare creature,*
*Will live forever in eternity.*

*The cross is never so close to a man,*
*'Til he humps where legions tread.*
*A painful stake was nailed to his hand,*
*Ten years later he arose from the dead.*

*Now the grunt parson did not really die,*
*Like a buddy once told a friend,*
*Shrapnel exploded between his eyes,*
*And his fate was cast to the wind.*

*The eighties arrived, the cause is lost,*
*The blood had dried away.*
*The paddy preacher had paid the cost,*
*And still had a little to pay.*

PHIL WOODALL, *RHYMER IN THE SUNSET*

# Assistant Chaplains

I had a bunch of great chaplain's assistants. For a long time in the military, I absolutely marveled to think that I had something like an assistant chaplain. Other chaplains didn't like the term, but I always did because that's what they were: assistant chaplains. Most of these guys felt keenly for the chaplain and protected him at all costs in the Nam. My thinking was that if these guys could be chaplain's assistants and not become disillusioned with the faith, it would be nothing short of a small miracle.

People have different views about the clergy, too often putting them on some kind of pedestal. For many of us, feet of clay is more like it. I viewed a chaplain's assistant as a little like a wife. The outside world might see the minister one way—think he's holier-than-thou, perhaps, but the wife sees him as he is. The chaplain's assistant definitely sees him as he is, warts and all.

My first assistant in Vietnam was the assistant for the chaplain before me and was Catholic. He was a super young troop and more than an assistant; he was a grunt at heart. He was a good soldier and got involved in firefights and heavy-duty action and had some definite ideas about how the chaplains in the Nam should act.

After he left, I never had another official chaplain's assistant—a 71M (that's the job title, the MOS-military occupational specialty). Most of my assistants were on-the-job training. Mostly, they were guys who needed to get out of the field for various reasons. I remember one especially. Let's call him Vic. What a study! Everybody called him Padre because, according to the troops, Vic was all into Jesus, and although most of them thought he was a little crazy, nobody messed with him. He was a terrific soldier, though he kept saying, "Jesus and killing—don't make no sense."

One story about Vic was that he collided head-on with an AK-47 and lived to tell about it. Ammunition from an

AK-47 travels between 900 to 1000 miles per hour, and a head-on collision at 60 miles per hour in a vehicle will kill nearly anyone if the car doesn't have airbags. Vic's head must have twisted around at least four times when he was hit by a fast-moving AK bullet. Fellow soldiers who witnessed the shot could hardly believe it. It knocked him right into a rice paddy. Dead for sure, everyone thought, but they discovered he was alive and unconscious. Someone pulled him out of the paddy, where he would have drowned. He was bleeding from the back of the neck where one bullet had exploded and exited. At least a third of his head should have been blown off. One of the medics, when patching him up, put a large stick straight through the two holes—one in the steel pot (helmet) and the other where the bullet had exited.

After he got out of the hospital, Vic simply could not bring himself to think of returning to the field, so we found a way for him be a chaplain's assistant.

After that a whole bevy of guys just hung around. I think they told people they were my assistants, but they didn't perform any real duties for me. Most ended up on the sergeant major's details, and there were always lots of duties: burning the feces, building something, hauling supplies, anything. They weren't out there facing "Sir Charles." Because we had a fairly extended time at Sandy and it looked like this was going to be our transition area, many of them hoped they could end up at Sandy waiting for that elusive trip south and home. The original 101st, at least the 2d and 3d brigades, had come over from Campbell in December, so that meant that they'd be rotating out the next December. I joined them in May, so in a sense I had six months with the original crew, or at least those who were left. They had lots of history at Campbell and also lost a lot of people in Nam.

Years later, my daughter Meg went to Vanderbilt in Nashville and I'd see her about once a month. Often, we went to a great restaurant out by the airport called Headquarters, 101st Airborne Division. The restaurant decor was set up exactly like you would imagine a headquarters in World War II. There were some old military vehicles, bales of hay, old communication equipment.

With regularity during these visits, I would ride up to Fort Campbell, Kentucky, and drink in a few memories. Without fail, I would feel the pall that often fell over the little community of Clarksville, Tennessee, and Hopkinsville, Kentucky, during Vietnam and now Iraq.

## The 101st

The 101st is one of those fabled units, and much of its glory dates back to World War II. In Vietnam, the 101st lost some of its legacy as it moved from being a paratrooper unit to an air mobility unit, and many troopers joining the 101st didn't have the sense of the history made by previous 101st warriors. In the D-day invasion, the 101st lost hundreds of men, and it lost hundreds more in Vietnam. They suffered through the deaths of 248 soldiers in 1985 when a plane crashed at Gander, Newfoundland, while returning home from a peacekeeping mission in the Sinai. Now, with more troops lost in Iraq, life remains extremely difficult for the surrounding little towns of Clarksville, Tennessee, and Hopkinsville, Kentucky. These two towns are made up mostly of military or ex-military families.

# *Rendezvous with Destiny*

The 101st Airborne Division, which was activated on August 16, 1942, at Camp Claiborne, Louisiana, has no history, but it has a rendezvous with destiny. Like the early American pioneers whose invincible courage was the foundation stone of this nation, we have broken with the past and its traditions to establish our claim to the future.

Due to the nature of our armament and the tactics in which we shall perfect ourselves, we shall be called upon to carry out operations of far-reaching military importance and we shall habitually go into action when the need is immediate and extreme.

The history we shall make, the record of high achievement we hope to write in the annals of the American Army and the American people, depends wholly and completely on the men of this Division. Each individual, each officer and each enlisted man must therefore regard himself as a necessary part of a complex and powerful instrument for the overcoming of the enemies of the nation. Each, in his own job, must realize that he is not only a means, but an indispensable means for obtaining the goal of victory. It is, therefore, not too much to say that the future itself, in whose moulding we expect to have a share, is in the hands of the soldiers of the 101st Airborne Division.

GENERAL WILLIAM C. LEE,
FATHER OF THE AMERICAN AIRBORNE

*Some people come into our lives and
quickly go. Some stay for a while and leave
footprints on our hearts,
and we are never, ever the same again.*

FLAVIA

# A Family at Home
# and a Family at War

There is a concept that after being away from home for eight or nine months, the people you're with become your primary family and your family at home becomes your secondary one. It makes sense—the camaraderie of the troops, the life and death existence, every day out there doing your thing. Fortunately, I think, we didn't understand this concept when we were in the Nam. Only when we returned home and attempted to cope with what someone has called a type of arrested development did we begin to understand the closeness and brotherhood of soldiers, especially combat soldiers. The treatment by family and friends and neighbors often traumatized returning Vietnam vets more than the war had, and many regressed.

The vast majority of Vietnam vets moved on with their lives. Most of us came back with some adjustment problems but better coping skills, and education and family support helped us. But many did not have the emotional resources to proceed with their lives.

Even today, many Vietnam combat troops still are struggling. They give life a good shot, but they can't handle it. They still are grieving. I see it all the time. Recently, I was on a city bus and noticed a guy wearing a VA hospital bracelet. Our eyes locked for a second and I nodded and said, "Vietnam vet." I quizzed him a little—11B with the first CAV; probably had been in Phuoc Vinh and Quan Loi near Cambodia. He was pretty reluctant to talk, so I let him return to his thousand-yard stare.

Some vets try in almost inane ways to return to Vietnam or at least to the bonding they felt there. They dress in their old fatigues and wear patches and badges. They show up at parades and dedications—anything to give them some release from Vietnam. Every time someone criticizes them, especially other vets, for looking like a ragtag band of rejects, I want to deck the vet who's criticizing, who was lucky enough to have moved on.

## The Community at Home

How families at home relate to vets is a much more complex issue. In a sense, it is almost impossible for them to relate. I remember seeing the movie *The War at Home* with Emilio Estevez as a returning vet. The family could not understand why he couldn't move on. Dealing with his bizarre behavior became almost imossible. *Jackknife*, with Robert DeNiro, dealt with some of the same issues.

My own family was incredibly supportive when I was in Vietnam and my wife's family was immensely so. But it was still hard, and in many ways it became even harder when we returned.

Another whole segment is the never-ending grief for those left behind. Books could be filled with stories of those whose loved ones died in Vietnam; their lives have been immeasurably affected and continue to be.

> Dear Abby,
> My boyfriend is a Marine. When he was fighting in Iraq, he sent me e-mails saying how much he missed me and loved me. When he came home, he was a completely different person. He was sent back to Iraq. He is back home but more distant than ever, I don't think he loves me. What should I do?

I think of all these families who are losing loved ones in Iraq. It is very different now as there is much support for the troops. Vietnam taught us to separate the war from the warrior, but still, for those families who lose loved ones in Iraq or Afghanistan, when the fanfare fades, the families will be alone in their grief, and often grieving the loss of a son or daughter in war means suffering alone. A person who has not gone through that particular sort of pain can say they identify with it, but it's not so. They want to understand out of kindness but they really don't. It's sad for all.

A good friend of mine still grieves for her brother who died in Vietnam. She was sixteen when he was killed. Her parents didn't know how to include her in the grief.

They were too busy trying to save themselves, which they weren't able to do. She lost her best friend—a great brother—and she wasn't allowed to grieve. It has affected her entire life, and in a sense, her grieving came much, much later—30 years later. A really good friend of mine told me that when his brother was killed in Vietnam, his mom went into the house and didn't come out for seven years.

*The long shadows of the past fade*
*and stretch from now to then*
*but the shadows in my mind*
*and in my heart are also fading.*

NELSON DEMILLE, *UPCOUNTRY*

# Colonel, I Guess It Was Me

Coming back to Sandy from the field, I always felt a certain amount of elation. I had been tested in combat. I hadn't done much but I was there. However, I can now admit that all the accusations that I took on the persona of an infantryman are true. As I look back, I don't know what I would have done differently, given the circumstances. The troops were always glad to see me. I could do the same things they did. In a sense, I was extra help. On a deeper level, maybe I made what they did—the killing, the combat—more palatable because I was doing it, too. I don't know, and I'm conflicted about it to this day. Waxing philosophical in the comfort of my living room and being on the battlefield are not the same, obviously—one can't be morphed into the other.

179

My hairiest experience, however, occurred not in the field but at Sandy. When I think about it, my adrenalin starts pumping. It was war—constant combat, always on the ready and always expecting. Had I not been a good combat soldier, I, and many others, might not have lived to tell this tale.

The days passed and dark set in and I was in and out of the field as usual. The commander was always good-naturedly ribbing me, especially when he couldn't find me. "Chaplain," he'd say, "it's hard to hit a moving target." When I was at the FSB, I was always a little restless and wanted to be in the field. There was something about the FSB that made me always on the ready and on edge!

This particular day, I came from the field around dark, dropped off by a "log" (logistics) bird that had resupplied one of the companies. I felt more than the usual apprehension. Company B had been engaged in a prolonged firefight. We were pinned down for a couple of hours. What made this firefight seem especially tough was constant harassing fire from a tree line. No amount of artillery or any kind of suppressing fire could halt the occasional burst. Imagine the shaking of heads when we finally got the VC: we found an old man operating an 82mm machine gun—chained to it. He was dug in behind a whole row of trees. He could fire and not be seen, and he could not escape. We'd heard the VC did such things, but this was the first time we'd seen it. I was still on edge.

I wrote my letter to Jackie and read a little. My mouth felt like cotton and I was sweating. *Get hold of yourself, boy*, I said to myself, mocking my dad, who had always called me boy. "Boy, get in the car. Boy, get in some stove wood." My dad was such a great guy and his "boy" was a term of affection.

Everybody seemed to be asleep. I knew Sandy like the back of my hand. In my mind's eye, I had memorized every crack and cranny. At night when I was in camp, I visited every soldier on the LPs (lookouts were called listening posts—LPs—at night and OPs in the daytime). I knew where the *fougasse* (a French term for napalm in barrels, kind of like a Molotov cocktail) was, and claymore mines were lethal at 50 to 75 yards. I counted the tents and knew exactly who was in them, other than a few transient soldiers who were passing through on their way south. I knew who smoked pot and where they got it and how to catch them and keep them off guard duty. I could smell pot a mile away—an aptitude that is still with me.

We had good security: an Ops NCO, usually supervised by the sergeant major, along with a couple of senior NCOs providing the details (the tasks that soldiers hate—things that are routine, like pulling guard, burning the feces; in the old days it would have been KP—kitchen police). Despite our good security, I never felt really safe and never figured out why other than I was in Vietnam and we were at war.

I had walked down to the TOC earlier and looked around. I sat for a while listening to the radio traffic. There was sporadic contact in the AO, but overall it seemed quiet. Outside, it was dark and I was wishing for morning. I hate the dark and in Vietnam the dark is like dark nowhere else. It always unnerved me. It would be pitch-dark right up to the moment before first light, and then it was as though someone had turned on a switch. Dark to light was immediate.

My thoughts were running together, I couldn't focus; my mouth was still dry. *Settle down,* I told myself. *This is like being in the rear.* Something was going to happen—I just knew it. We might get mortared. What about sappers? (Sappers were VC who got inside the perimeter and committed suicide while killing and creating havoc.)

I decided to walk around some more. My heart was racing. I went into the tent and picked up a hand flare. SFC Henry had taught me well. We had practiced firing hand flares a couple of times when we were at the firing range at the Special Forces camp in Bien Hoa. I remember him saying, "You can't fire at something unless you can see it." I always had flares around. I made sure a clip was in my weapon and chambered a round. *I am crazy.*

When I walked back outside, I thought I caught something in the corner of my eye—someone crouching down. *Just imagining.* I stopped, knelt down, and was sure I saw a silhouetted figure slightly outlined against the sky about four tents down. He was crouched and sitting like only a Vietnamese can sit. I moved slightly behind the corner of a tent. He didn't move. *Patience.* I was still watching. *What about whispering a challenge?* I thought. We had a password, but I didn't know it and nobody ever paid any attention to them. I kind of whispered, "What's the password?" expecting an answer. A GI could at least say, "I don't know."

I popped a hand flare and screamed out, *la dai, la dai* (come) and let go with a burst from my weapon. I screamed like I'd never screamed before, "Sappers, sappers!" A grenade went off. Time stopped. I wasn't breathing, but somehow I managed to fire off another hand flare. Suddenly, someone cut loose with a sixteen and somebody else shot off several more flares. Three figures sprinted toward the fence. VC. The LPs cut loose, and then a sixty was barking and they went down. It was silent for a moment—no movement.

The artillery battery illuminated the whole area. Thank God for those redlegs. It was as light as day, and four more figures scampered across in the open. A whole gaggle of GIs fired on full automatic. Somebody yelled, "They're behind the supply tent." I saw a figure dart and somebody fired from another direction. Suddenly there was a big explosion. Something or somebody blew up like a bomb. Eighty-two-millimeter mortars were walking their way along the berm and 4.2s (mortars) followed them.

By this time, the whole area was bathed in flares and it was as bright as day. Several troops moved toward the supply tent, where a fire was blazing. The siren was howling and the place had come to life. The LPs were reporting that a couple of VC had been caught in the wire. The sappers had killed two GIs from the signal section. It could have been a disaster. There were eight dead VC, each with at least two satchel charges. They were just the advanced contingent, probably—no telling what could have happened. A lone VC, who appeared to have been heading toward the TOC, was dead. A dozen grenades were strapped to his body and he had a map of several tents surrounding the TOC. He probably knew the layout of the TOC and would have wreaked havoc, not to mention killing everyone who was working as well as the commander.

A well-designed sapper attack sent in an advance party to blow up the ammo tent and the command section and everything they could get to. For the sappers, it was considered a suicide mission. They were paving the way for an NVA unit or a larger VC force and could have annihilated everyone in the fire support base. It didn't happen to us that night, but it came close.

I was shaking so hard, I didn't know what to do. I went into the tent and somehow made it for the few remaining hours to dawn. The next morning, I was out of Sandy on the first chopper to one of the companies. I needed to get my head together.

*The day that will live in infamy—*
*no, not Pearl Harbor. April 30, 1975. The*
*day that Marines fought with screaming*
*and crying Vietnamese, American Embassy*
*files burned in the courtyard, the city of*
*Saigon in chaos. The American Ambassador*
*carrying the folded flag—*
*a day that will live in infamy.*

STUDENT AT COMMAND AND GENERAL STAFF COLLEGE,
FORT LEAVENWORTH, KANSAS

# The Grand Experiment
# May Not Be for Everybody

Exporting democracy is a renowned political policy and bureaucratic wonks love to talk about it, but I'm not so sure that it is for everybody. Nation-building. What is that? There's ample evidence that American-style democracy simply may not be best for all the world.

In a sense, modern-day Vietnam is an example. From everything I read and from talking with Americans who've recently traveled to Vietnam—vets and others—for all practical purposes Vietnam has become a capitalist society but still calls itself communist. This is not to downplay the challenges that American businessmen or others have in doing business with a communist nation, but it is mostly bureaucracy. Evidence shows that life without war in Vietnam is not all bad and things are getting done.

Over half the populace was not even born during the Vietnam war. Most people I've talked to who have visited Vietnam recently say there are few reminders of what Vietnamese call the "American war." I've been involved for the last several years with a group of American pioneers called *Room to Read* that builds schools in Vietnam. The schools get built, using Room to Read's unique system, because the Vietnamese want schools for their kids. We help with the money, and they do the work, the planning, and the execution. It's pretty inspirational.

It's a delicate situation when American soldiers are in a foreign country. After serving in places like Vietnam, Korea, and Germany, I come down on the side of not engaging with the local culture. If we are going to assist countries in repelling a more aggressive country taking over a smaller one, which is how we started in Vietnam, we need to make that our mission and then move out. In the early stages of Nam, our moral purpose seemed admirable. When that purpose became obscured or overridden by other purposes, the job went awry. Exporting democracy is not a clean business. War is simply messy, and its aftermath is usually worse. Vietnam is still in our psyche and will be for the foreseeable future.

Toward the end of my tour, I debated the idea of our involvement in Vietnam with one of the chaplain's assistants. He never came right out and said he downright opposed what we were doing, but he presented a sort of passive resistance that I found admirable. For soldiers who made it toward the end in Vietnam, the illusion of fighting for a cause crumbled into the dust. Maybe we weren't the guys on the white horses. Maybe we shouldn't be in Vietnam. What if we've done all this for nothing? But GIs didn't lay those sixteens down; they dedicated themselves to getting the hell out of Nam in one piece. I think it probably happened to me. In a sense, I quit thinking about what I was doing and starting counting the days—*Do the job and get on to the next world.* Go home and forget it.

> *I understand why I am over here. The children do not deserve to live the way they are now or, even worse, the way they did before. They are so innocent and the only ones to wave and smile and cheer as we go through on patrols. You can see the cutoff and when they are pretty much brainwashed, because any child older than, I'd say, 9 or 10, will no longer wave or smile. But the children 8 and younger have no idea and they absolutely love us.*
>
> A YOUNG 82D AIRBORNE
> LIEUTENANT IN IRAQ

By this time in my experience, I had Vietnam sized up. I had become a good soldier and knew that issues like Vietnamization and winning the hearts and minds of the people were more a joke than anything else. And my powers of observation, especially of Vietnam's army that we saw, led me to know that we were never going to win their hearts.

Being out in the field with the ARVNs (Army of the Republic of Vietnam) could be incredibly disheartening. Our soldiers felt it and had written them off. It was not that they were bad people, but that this had simply become an American war. It was what the GIs believed and it was what the Vietnamese believed. We always had a few ARVNs with us, and what most GIs will remember them for is their cruelty to their own people and chasing down ducks or whatever they could find to eat in villages we trudged through.

One of the few times I ever intervened in anything involving the ARVNs was when a platoon trapped a couple of young boys who were definitely VC. They had been down a spider hole and somebody threw a Willy Peter in on them. This is a phosporus grenade that burns. I wasn't there when it happened but showed up on a normal "round," as I called it. The ARVNs had these young kids stripped down naked and stretched out and were beating the soles of their feet. They had already drawn blood. I stopped it. The lieutenant didn't look pleased. I pulled him aside and reamed him out a little. I told him that it was not right, not good for our soldiers to see, that and if these VC knew something, which I doubted, we could get it another way. Americans, I said, didn't do things this way. He grinned like I was his dad scolding him.

GIs had lost faith in their cause in Nam and this, if for no other reason, made it psychologically a losing endeavor. I still believe that we didn't lose the war, never lost a battle, and why should we?—we were good soldiers and had the fire power. We lost the war for reasons far beyond the lowly GI (myself included), not in the rice paddies of Nam but the halls of Congress, with distorted media reporting, the "perfect storm" concept, election to Congress of many antiwar types, and so on. For the soldier, it became a matter of individual survival: *Do the time and get the hell out.*

These were some of the things that Mark, chaplain's assistant extraordinaire, was saying. He was an E7 (sergeant first class) and I think one of the absolute best in terms of sizing it all up—"getting it." Technically, he should not have been with me as an E7, but it was one of those expediency things. I probably was the only one who would have him because of his strident views. He wouldn't go to the field. I could care less as I didn't need him looking after me anyway.

Mark came to me in a somewhat unusual way. We had been at Bragg together. I didn't really know him well but liked what I remembered. At Bragg, the home of the Airborne, he looked the part, was in great physical condition and a master blaster (master parachutist)— meaning he was somewhat of a lifer, as the troops said. The division chaplain, however, chafed under his raucous views about Vietnam.

To be honest, I didn't know which end was up half the time in terms of protocol or how things were supposed to work in the military—issues like control and who was in charge totally eluded me. But they were on top of somebody's list, and the good sergeant first class chaplain's assistant came to reside with me.

Soon after he came to me, I was out with B Company, whose point man, Johnson, was a long, tall, skinny black kid I'd nurtured and coaxed into going back to the field. Why? Well, I thought at the time he needed to do it for himself, and I was out there to give him support. I found out Johnson had been killed in the morning. The lieutenant had insisted that he didn't want him to walk point but Johnson insisted. *Oh, God!* He was killed by a lone sniper. I knelt over his body beside a hedgerow and prayed.

When I returned to Sandy that afternoon, my replacement was waiting for me. He handed me a note from the division chaplain that said something like, "No argument: you have a few weeks left, you're going south." I left that afternoon for Bien Hoa to finish out my time in the Nam. My new chaplain's assistant was waiting for me. Life with my new assistant was easier. In the good sergeant's mind, we were away from the war. The assistant was a super scrounger and could get anything. He made an arrangement with the PX in Bien Hoa by which all damaged goods were turned over to the chaplain section. We gave it to Ma and Pa Kincaid, two wonderful American missionaries in Saigon. They ran a school for kids and took on social service projects like an activity center for teens, trying desperately to keep young girls out of the clutches of prostitution. It was a losing battle.

Ma and Pa Kincaid deserve a book of their own—explaining why they made the sacrifices and put themselves in danger. I discovered a good bit about my own church's missionary system, too. Missionaries from more affluent church denominations didn't seem to be nearly as ferocious in serving the people. For the Kincaids, it was all about service. If they had any worldly possessions, I surely didn't see them.

The few other missionaries I saw or came to know—in Saigon, in particular—lived in really nice houses, had servants, and didn't make much of a difference with the people. This sounds harsh, but I compared other missionaries to Ma and Pa Kincaid, and the others didn't measure up. After Vietnam fell, my efforts to find out what happened to them met with little success. I think they probably stayed behind, and if they survived, lived out their lives among the people they loved and served.

> *When Sitting Bull toured with Buffalo Bill's Wild West circus, he gave his earnings to the street urchins he encountered, appalled that a society that could produce such wealth could permit such poverty.*
>
> UNKNOWN

*Every person born into this world*
*represents something new,*
*something that never existed before,*
*something original and unique . . .*

MARTIN BUBER, *THE WAY OF MAN*

# Nothing Is Too Good
# for the Soldier, and That Is
# Usually What He Gets—Nothing

"The needs of the Army" is one of those catch phrases that means, in soldier terms, "Screw over the soldier." Most chaplains view themselves as the soldier's advocate. I did. In Nam, I saw weird things over and over in the name of "military needs." McNamara's 100,000 is but one example. To give the planners their due, some things worked surprisingly well. For example, to make up for a shortage before the 101st left Fort Campbell, they had to import some soldiers since there weren't enough infantry to go around. Therefore, they brought in some

MPs from Bragg and suddenly they were eleven bravos (infantrymen)—amazing.

I remember two of those guys. Although they were not in the same company, they were fast friends, carrying on a running dialogue no matter where they were. One got to be a sergeant first and never let his buddy forget it.

Soldiers had rituals—superstitions. Doug, one of these guys, had an amazing fear of getting hit with friendly fire. When the artillery FO (forward observer) prepared to call in fire, he insisted on checking the coordinates. This created friction, and once they even had a fistfight that I had to break up. Doug taught me how to read a map. The ability to find your exact location and convert it to grid coordinates could save your life.

In combat, there is almost no sound as welcome as that of your own artillery whizzing over your head en route to pound an enemy. Unfortunately, as good as friendly fire can be, with hundreds of actions going on at any one time with all kinds of players, we kill our own troops more often than we like to admit.

To be hit by friendly fire was the most dreaded happenstance in Vietnam. Most units had an FO . This was an artillery lieutenant, sometimes with an NCO and his radio telephone operator wired into a firing artillery battery. The battery was usually a 155 howitzer or a 105—a weapon that could deliver an awesome payload. The artillery batteries delivered with great accuracy, but on occasion, with wrong coordination mainly, friendly fire became a nightmare.

In the Nam, nothing caused sheer panic more than the sudden realization that your own artillery was coming in on top of you. We had some pretty bad incidents, most never reported. There seemed to be an unwritten rule that friendly fire was the absolute worst way to be killed—*Let the enemy get me but not my own people.* The fact that either way one is dead seemed to have no significance to soldiers in combat. The unwritten rule was: *If an individual is killed by friendly fire, it was the VC.* Soldiers in Nam wanted the feeling that they died for a purpose, and to die by the enemy's hand was infinitely better than your own troops killing you.

Friendly fire is part of being a soldier. Despite the best efforts of all involved, it will happen from time to time. Doug's mantra was, "No way am I being killed by my own people." At least the military chain of command in Iraq seems to have learned from prior mistakes like Vietnam: tell it like it is and move on.

Were we wrong to cover up many friendly-fire incidents as we did in Vietnam? If treated properly, in the long run, families might have felt better knowing the truth. Maybe not. I am not sure anything could make a loved one's death palatable in a war so muddled as Vietnam.

*I was thinking—in all these years we've been*
*married, you've never once said you were sorry.*

EDITH BUNKER

*I'll gladly say I'm sorry*
*if I ever say anything wrong.*

ARCHIE BUNKER

# How Many Angels Can Stand
# on the Head of a Pin?

Ministry in Vietnam still amazes me now, going on 40 years after I was there. I think of the chaplain buddies I knew—a real cast of characters. At any one time, there might have been 2,000 chaplains in Vietnam. Until recently, the military recognized only three basic religious groups: Protestants, Catholics and Jews. Recently, we've taken in Muslim chaplains.

I was totally opposed to incorporating Muslims into the official structure of the chaplaincy, mainly because I didn't think it was needed. Needless to say, the chief of chaplains never asked me. Chaplains in the military had served Muslims for a long time just as they had every other group, and they had done it without changing the basic structure that had existed from almost the very beginning. We easily could have contracted with civilian Muslim clergy for their work. For years we had been serving the black Muslim movement in the Army—the Nation of Islam. But the Chief of Chaplain's Office has not been known as a bastion of original thinkers and, like much of the military before 9/11, the idea of multiculturalism trumped ministry and almost everything else. What we have discovered since then is that when several chiefs of chaplains rushed to be politically correct, inadequate safeguards on motives may have contributed to some embarrassing and possibly dangerous situations relating to the present war on terrorism.

On the surface, it would almost appear that the idea of having chaplaincy in the military is nigh unto impossible. The idea that you could get that many clergy cooperating on anything is beyond imagination. There are some givens, naturally. Catholics serve Catholics with their whole sets of theology: canon law and all that is specific to their church. Rabbis do the same in terms of Judaism and base their services on their brand of Judaism: Reform, Conservative, or Orthodox. But priests and rabbis also serve soldiers in other religions, or would in a variety of ways if they were called upon or if their help was needed. It happened all the time and still does. No priest or rabbi I've known would refuse to help a soldier or anybody else in the military with any problem, even one unrelated to a faith issue.

At one time, there were more than 139 Protestant denominations. Surprisingly, in Vietnam they not only cooperated but did wonderful things in support of each other. Chaplains sometimes had differences based on theology or church polity, but these were relatively minor. For instance, the Mormons were known for proselytizing; most Lutherans didn't like participating in worship services with other chaplains; the Episcopalians wanted their liturgy. But as far as serving the soldier was concerned, Protestants cooperated.

I cannot imagine a chaplain refusing to serve the soldier because he or she was not of their particular church. To a chaplain, this would be ridiculous. It's rare that faith issues cause a chaplain's lack of enthusiasm; it's more likely that he's lazy, overworked, disinterested, or has personality problems.

The Protestant chaplain in particular has always been the poor man's psychiatrist. Soldiers can walk into the chaplain's office or stop him anytime, anywhere, and ask for help. For most of the military, especially the soldier, the chaplain is the first line of emotional defense.

I always had lots of friends who were priests and was intrigued by them. The idea of not knowing women, in the Biblical sense, was a little strange, and I was not above some good-natured teasing. In my experience, it just seemed that many of them were like me—a little weird. Celibacy may have worked for many; however, the few priests I knew more than casually and who were my good buddies seemed to ignore the whole celibacy thing. Whether or not they came to realize celibacy was a bad proposition or that it simply didn't work, I don't have a hint. Maybe they just got to know us Protestant heretics too well and figured that marriage or women were a better alternative. For years, we joked, with more truth than fiction, that we knew several priests whose housekeepers' children looked remarkably like them. For most Protestant types, this was a long way from condemnation—rather, we felt, "More power to them."

Rudy (not his real name) was one of my good priest buddies. He was an artillery chaplain. Every infantry battalion had one battery that supported the unit. My unit had a battery of four 105 howitzers. From time to time, Father Rudy, who covered all of the artillery, would show up. We'd chat, laugh, and tell a few war stories. Most of the time, if I was around (which wasn't often), Rudy hassled me by saying, "We call you the Howard Hughes of the Chaplain Corps. We've heard you exist but nobody's ever seen you." My retort was that I was not like the rest of these REMF chaplains, I was out with the troops. It was jovial banter, and we enjoyed it.

On rare occasions, we'd sit around the mess tent with Louie and drink his wicked Raisin Jack. After about half a cup I could hardly see my feet. It was so incredibly deceptive: sweet, delightful, and powerful. I didn't do it often because I hated to be out of control. I don't know that I ever thought about it that deeply at the time, but I can tell you this; the last place in the world that you wanted to be out of control was Vietnam.

## Hospitality Plus

Rudy was bald and looked like a friar. He was a little pudgy, but a fabulous guy and I liked him immensely. When I went to Camp Eagle, the upcountry division headquarters, I always stopped in. He had a nice hooch and liked to share the amenities that he could get that we line doggies couldn't—the little goodies that came to him because he was in the rear.

One incident at Rudy's place was one of those "you-had-to-be-there" experiences. A cherry chaplain had just come up from down south and was staying at Rudy's for a day or so. I think he was going to be the aviation chaplain. Other guys were constantly coming through Rudy's place—a regular menagerie of folks, which was the way he did things. Most priests were like this, I think. Since they didn't have wives and children, in the States they opened their homes to troops and families, and the practice carried over to Vietnam. Rudy loved to hobnob.

A young infantry captain was in the room and had laid his grease gun (like the small tommy gun Elliot Ness and the bad guys used during the Prohibition years) on one of the bunks. The weapon used 45-caliber bullets. The cherry chaplain casually picked up the grease gun to look it over and it went off (did I mention that tommy guns were known for having a hair trigger?) and fired several shots. It scared the daylights out of everybody. We all jumped like crazy. The first thing I knew, the young captain was out of there along with his weapon. The ashen-faced young chaplain had his head in his hands moaning, "Oh no, oh no." Rudy was bewildered. We were quiet for what seemed like an eternity, and then things around us seemed to get back to normal.

Rudy's tent was in a long row of officers' tents, and little pathways wound through them. Nobody said anything. We waited—nothing. Finally, I said, "I've got to be out of here." I was kind of amused in a way—this could have been a tragedy, but apparently nothing had happened. At least nobody showed up to question us or do anything. We weren't about to go announcing what had happened. I always did think that given all the weapons in Vietnam (every soldier had two or three), it was a wonder more of us weren't killed by other soldiers.

The postscript to this story was that apparently the bullets went through the tent, traveled about a hundred meters, and hit a soldier in the shoulder. Nobody knew where the shots had come from and the soldier was given a Purple Heart, since *obviously it must have been enemy fire.* In fact, I later heard from Rudy that the soldier got an infection, was sent south, then to a hospital in Japan, and then home. The shot heard that night probably saved his life. I never saw the young chaplain who was the perpetrator of the good deed again.

*There's no honorable way to kill,*
*no gentle way to destroy.*
*There's nothing good in war*
*except its ending.*

ATTRIBUTED TO ABRAHAM LINCOLN

# You Are Coming in Broken and Distorted

My usual schedule was being out with a company or even a platoon for most of the week and then coming in for Sunday services. Days were not delineated in Vietnam; they never are when you're at war. One day just runs into the next. Based on where we were, I'd have some sort of worship service every time I was with a company or platoon or squad. I always tried to be at the FSB on Sunday.

At Sandy, I had a medium tent with a nice altar—high cotton! We had a sergeant major who put a gigantic cross right in front of the chapel. It was huge and I often thought, *Well, guess the VC could zero in on this if they wanted to.*

This week was like all others, but I remember the beginning of it in particular. I was with B company. I remember that the company commander was a new guy and I didn't know him well, as he had been in the company for just a few weeks. Sometimes a new guy would look at me kind of befuddled, like *What or who is this?* I was older than most of the other officers by five or six years at least. They were just out of college or the Point. I had been to seminary and had pastored a church by the time I came into the Army.

I think this was the commander's second tour of duty. He was a little uptight. The AO (area of operations) was hot all over. It was nothing to have every company in enemy contact of some sort, often at the same time. And it was necessary for a commander to get his act together quickly. Some of them didn't last long. One day we'd have a company commander, the next he'd get hit—killed or wounded—and he'd be gone. Once, a new company commander went to the field on the log (logistics) bird and got killed before he made it to the headquarters part of the company.

I'll call this commander Bill. The couple of times I'd seen him, I wondered if he wasn't just a little over the edge. He was friendly enough, but I just had one of those feelings. It was very important to me that the company commander and men knew that I was loyal to everybody, knew how to keep confidences, and was not reporting to the battalion on anything I saw or found. Most of the time I found a way to spell this out to new people. I didn't want some commander or young trooper thinking that every time he saw me he had to be on his toes lest he mess up.

I kept confidences unless it was something that absolutely had to be handled. Rarely—only a couple of times—did I have to get command involved or put myself into a situation that was not my job, and when I did, it was very painful for me. I had to take drastic action once with one of my favorite senior NCOs. He was an alcoholic who was in charge of security in the rear. He'd been one of our platoon sergeants and was very good. However, when he got to Sally, he was constantly putting the troops at risk and setting a bad example. He was drunk more than he was sober, often asleep when he was supposed to be checking guard posts. When two of his soldiers were killed because of his possible drunken stupor, I took action and he was relieved from duty. He never forgave me.

There was a little lag time from when the previous company commander left and when Bill arrived. The previous commander was there only a short time and may have been relieved.

One of the real difficulties of Vietnam was the lack of consistency and basic mission essentials. B Company had a terrific commander. They lost him; then his replacement was killed immediately. They got another one and for some reason, he was relieved. And now here was another. The company had been hit pretty hard, and command and control seemed to be part of the problem. I felt for these young commanders. They had all these higher-ups looking at them—the division commander, the brigade and battalion commanders. And motives were often suspect, even at war. Making rank and getting a combat command under your belt was surely one of the check marks on the way to becoming a general. "I just want to do my job," I often heard these young commanders say.

The company really had been hit hard. The word going around was that things were "out of control." I knew the company well. I knew all the companies well—they were my parish. I knew most of the men's names and made it a point to spend time with those who were constantly rotating in and out. In many ways I was the one constant the troops had, especially guys who were the old timers when I arrived. I saw some leave, others come in. By virtue of my chaplaincy, I was a constant.

A curious phenomenon developed: The unit should have been cohesive—a vital team working together—but as the old-timers left, it became less so. Platoon members hardly knew each other, much less the others in the company. With rotations in and out, it was hard to keep the sort of unity that made for good soldiering. In some ways, this was the nature of the beast.

Loyalty needed to exist among the men in each company, platoon, and squad—and, to a lesser degree, even outside that small circle. The men needed to know someone was there saying, "I've got your back."

The lack of cohesiveness was what made Vietnam combat uniquely different, which was both good and bad from a tactical standpoint. Cohesion too quickly disappeared, and this had a negative effect on how we conducted life-and-death operations. More than was admitted, however, this aspect of the Vietnam war paved the way for a better future military, especially in terms of tactics. Many of Vietnam's young commanders who survived went on to become the leaders in the Army and brought along the lessons they'd learned in Vietnam. Let us hope this continues in Iraq as the war stretches out. Units need to be cohesive, not groups of individuals.

A problem that was rare with my battalion was pot. A combat soldier with his head messed up on weed is asking to die. Overall for our unit, drugs were not a problem. Movies like *Apocalypse Now* satirize the Vietnam experience and simply get it wrong—Vietnam was not about doped out soldiers stoned to the max. It may have been true in some of the rear units, but the amount of pot use has been exaggerated. Soldiers who were into dope had a tendency to say that all the soldiers were using it—this made them feel that their use was justified.

I had ways of checking on drug use and knew that it was not pervasive in our battalion. We were fighting constantly, and trying to stay alive leaves little time for anything else. I can't speak for other battalions, but I think dope was used more in units that were near the civilian populace than in those that had high enemy contact. Staying alive was more important than getting high! Most line soldiers were careful not to do dope or to be selective about when they did. For many, escaping the rigors of constant war was no small thing, and when there was a stand-down or a trip to Coco Beach, maybe they smoked.

After the loss of a commander, it was common practice to put soldiers in less dangerous situations so that they could recover, and guarding bridges was one of those less dangerous duties. Once, when B Company had been out on the bridges far too long, I think several men stocked up on weed. Bridge-guarding was an often boring job given to a unit that had seen a lot of action—a chance for a break. Civilians passing by were ready suppliers of the weed.

• • •

Back to Bill. The former commander had left, Bill had arrived to replace him, and he hadn't been around too long. Suddenly, one day, I heard him yelling and ran toward the scene. "If I catch you smoking dope and it jeopardizes any of us, I'll kill you myself," he screamed. He held a cocked 45 to a soldier's temple and had a wild look about him. I thought he was going to blow the trooper's head off. I didn't move, and after what seemed like an eternity, he released the hammer and walked away. I definitely remember that morning.

Soldiers loved to take communion during a lull in the fighting or anytime they could. When I announced we were having a service, almost everybody came. The services were short. Usually, I would read from the Bible or from a poem, give a short inspirational homily, say a prayer, and then offer communion. What I told them about communion was this: "Regardless of your tradition—or even if you don't have one—when you participate in the sacraments, this is your way of saying 'I believe,' that you trust in God, that this is your commitment."

Almost all of the troops took communion.

During Vietnam, I was a Baptist, and we didn't use the word "sacrament." But I realized that many of the men were Catholics or had other religious backgrounds in which the word "sacrament" was used. Taking the sacraments has different meanings to different denominations, but when you're at war, nobody pays attention to differences. I gave communion by intinction, which is dipping the wafer (if any were available) in the wine or juice. On occasion, I even used water.

A couple of times when we were having services, we were mortared or took fire. At least once that I remember, a priest was with me saying Mass, and suddenly we had an all-out attack. He was a great guy and I kidded him, saying, "This is the last time we're bringing you to the field."

Occasionally, I had a small tape recorder with tapes of some hymns and little hymnbooks to sing from. I gave the troops Bibles by the score and also gave them crosses or crucifixes they could wear. Troops would often ask me to bless them. In the beginning, I'd explain that I wasn't a priest. More than likely the soldier would say, "Would you bless it anyway?" I usually kissed the cross.

Sleep was always so distant. We would go for days without sleep, it seemed. And we were bone-tired. Sometimes I'd stay out eight or ten days, with daytime temperatures over 100 degrees. Our uniforms were always sweat-drenched and at night we froze.

Sometimes fresh water was unavailable. In our AO, we sometimes found bomb craters with water in them. We put awful-tasting purification tables in the water and hoped for the best. We had to be careful, though, because of the leeches. Once, I got one in my mouth—not a good experience. Other times, water was everywhere. We often slept with water over our legs, using our "steel pots" (helmets) for pillows. When the water began to get in our ears, we learned to sleep standing up.

We didn't see many tanks; seeing this one was a novelty. A *Hoi Chanh* sits beside me. This was the name given Vietnamese who joined the *Chieu Hoi* program for Vietcong who came over to our side. Most of the Hoi Chanh were young, and I got to know several of them. My favorite was called White Elephant. I don't remember the one next to me in this photo; I think we just wanted to be on a tank that day.

Being very positive for the troops was important to me; sometimes I smiled when it was the last thing I wanted to do. This photo was taken in a helicopter; the pilot is smiling behind me. These helicopter pilots were great. On a few occasions, I was assigned my own helicopter—once to fly around to all the troops at Christmas. For a short time, I felt like a big shot. So many of these brave pilots died; they often were cowboys in the best sense of the word. (I got to know one who loved to clip the trees when he took off!) They could set a chopper down amid withering fire to pick up the wounded, bring in ammo, or whatever else they were asked to do.

On one combat assault, the pilot motioned for us to jump when we were still about twelve feet off the ground. He thought we were closer because the elephant grass was about ten feet high and distorted his estimate. Jumping twelve feet while wearing a sixty-pound pack was a challenge. On another mission, we were put down over a rice paddy and almost drowned—we were mired up to our hips in mud.

On many nights, I visited observation posts like this one at the FSB (fire support base.) I felt it was necessary to check on the soldiers. I pretended I was their father, and few seemed to mind, and even if they did, I was there. The observation posts were designed to look toward the perimeters with a sharp eye for any enemy activity. What amazed me was how dark it could get in Vietnam and how darkness fell immediately. Nightfall was a dangerous time and many Vietnam vets suffer from PTSD that manifests itself as a fear of the dark. Many vets experience a rapid chain of flashbacks related to things that happened at night.

Chinook helicopters were most often used for delivering supplies or large numbers of troops. Rarely were they out in the fields of fire, but it happened sometimes. They kicked up an unbelievable amount of sand and dust. For a while afterwards, it was in everything. Worst of all, it got in our teeth and seemed to stay for days.

M ost of the time I was a happy guy at war. For me, as with many soldiers, war quickly became a way of life. Where else could a chaplain/minister/priest/rabbi be more needed than at war? The chaplain's flag signified "The chaplain is in." Anybody could walk in and see the chaplain.

This was my chaplain's tent, probably at the fire support base. It served as an office, sleeping quarters, and a place to meet with soldiers. I was there almost every Saturday and Sunday, although whether I was there depended on the operational missions that were going on. On occasion, I ended up with a platoon or company and could not get back to the base, so I stayed in the field.

Fire Support Base Sandy really was Sandy Star, right in the middle of nowhere it seemed, but very close to the beach. There were many rumors about the placement of FSP Sandy, mainly that during the Tet Offensive, many NVA (North Vietnam Army) troops had been trapped between the South China Sea and the city of Hue. Our battalion's job was to find them, and Sandy Star was right in the middle of their hideout. Our unit did find scores of the NVA hiding out as civilians or underground.

The city of Hue. Once it must have been a beautiful city. But it was no longer beautiful after the Tet offensive, which most believe was the turning point of Americans' view of the war. Although the NVA took heavy casualties and were decisively defeated, the public began to perceive the Vietnam situation as an ever-widening war from which no good would come. I loved Hue and as I traveled through it many times, I met some wonderful Vietnamese and American nuns called the Sisters of Mercy. Their dedication was amazing. When they needed a vehicle, my unit collected money and bought one for them.

There is no more difficult time for a soldier than holidays. Christmas was especially hard. I tried to visit every company on Christmas Day. Someone sent this little Christmas tree to me and I took it to all the companies so they would all have a Christmas tree, even if only for a little while. At one company, an incredibly sad event marred the day. Supposedly, a Christmas truce had been declared, but one of the lieutenants walked outside the perimeter of the camp and stepped on a booby trap. He was killed instantly. Death was always sad but a death happening on Christmas Day caused much reflection. I arrived just after it happened and conducted a memorial service. The lieutenant had been in-country for only a few weeks, and I had met him when he came to the FSB en route to his company. Like most young lieutenants heading off into the unknown, he had seemed dazed. It was so sad.

The sign in this photo is misspelled. There was a young GI who worked in the supply section—one I had bailed out of a jam with one of the sergeant majors—and he was determined to do something nice for me. He made the sign, and I never had the heart to tell him that he had misspelled chaplain.

When we established FSB Sandy Star the sergeant major asked me if we needed a chapel. I said of course we did. On his own, he decided we needed the gigantic cross shown in the picture. I always joked about the size and the fact that it could be a great target for the VC. We didn't have many politically correct types in the war zone in those days. I cannot remember a single time anyone ever said anything about the cross. Had it been up to me, we probably wouldn't have had the cross, but for whatever reason, the sergeant major wanted it. During my time in Vietnam, I was the chaplain for Jews, Catholics, Protestants, atheists or whatever, as were all the chaplains who served, I believe. We might have had different styles of ministry, but we were inclusive.

For the last month or so that I was in Vietnam, I was slightly wounded and sent south to be the chaplain for SERTS (Screaming Eagle Replacement Training School). We were at Bien Hoa and kids were everywhere. This photo was taken at a Catholic orphanage.

We frequently saw "buffalo boys" sitting a couple of hundred meters away from us. Most of the time, they were just kids. But occasionally, we discovered that they were mapping out our position to pass on to the VC.

Humping the boonies was a constant for the infantrymen. These guys carried a rucksack with five days of rations, a poncho, extra socks if they could get them, bug juice (insect repellant), a first aid kit, a blanket, ten magazine rounds for their M16 rifle, 100 rounds of ammo if they were machine-gunners, three claymore mines, eight trip flares and a trip wire, six smoke canisters, eight grenades, several packs of C4 explosives, and sometimes 10 rounds of M79 grenade launcher ammo. Each platoon carried a starlight scope to enable them to see at night. All of this could weigh between 60 to 100 pounds per man.

Sadly, when a soldier was killed or seriously injured, often it was impossible for a chopper to land and pick him up. The troops would take turns carrying the body and the soldier's load, often miles, to get to an LZ. Sometimes, they would have to make an LZ by cutting trees and bushes so the "bird" could get in and pick up the soldier.

*To those who sold doves he said,*
*"Get these out of here! How dare you turn*
*my Father's house into a market"!*

JOHN 2:16

*He has made everything beautiful*
*in its time. He has also set eternity in the*
*hearts of men; yet they cannot fathom what*
*God has done from beginning to end.*

ECCLESIASTES 3:11

# Ah, Man's Little Pleasures —or not

A couple of hours after the incident with Bill, I got a call from the Divarty (division artillery) general's aide-de-camp wanting to know if I'd seen the good Father Rudy.

"No, not in a few weeks," I replied.

"Well, the general is trying to locate him and said that he's signed out to be with your unit."

What could I say—*You're coming in broken and distorted?* When I had time to collect my thoughts, I covered for Rudy. "Well, I haven't seen him, but that doesn't mean he's not out here—sometimes he is and I don't know where. When I see him, I'll tell him you're looking for him." This was relatively true. Rudy did often say mass for the troops if the brigade Catholic chaplain wasn't available or if we couldn't find him, which happened with some regularity.

The general's aide was persistent. "Chaplain, I don't think you understand. The general wants him now."

Asshole. "You're coming in broken and distorted," I said. "I'll see if I can find him." I basically forgot all about it and shortly got another call, this time from a major who said, somewhat irritated, "Where is Father Rudy? The General wants to know now."

I said in my head, *To hell with the general—just because he wants him doesn't mean he has to pop out of a hat. We're trying to do a job.* "Say again. You're coming in broken and distorted." At the very least I could pretend I never got the request. We were at war and men were being killed, and I had more important things to do than find Father Rudy. The major came on again, sort of threatening. What an asshole. "Sorry, sir, you are coming in broken and distorted," I said. Then I broke contact.

What a great thing! Anytime you didn't want to get all wrapped around the axle with somebody, the old "broken and distorted" ploy was the best. *Thank you, Lord!*

• • •

The general continued to have people call about Rudy, and the urgency of the calls seemed a little weird. I didn't think much about it, but then somebody said Louie wanted to see me. He had come out with the supply chopper to serve his hot meal. I usually got a charge out of his attire, but today he just looked weary and overweight. "What's up, my man?" I said.

"Chaplain, I've got a problem and need you to come in with me."

"Sure, what's going on?"

"Well, rather not talk about here but believe me, big problem."

I hopped on the chopper and we touched down a few minutes later at Sandy. We walked back to the mess tent, taking a shortcut past a couple of 105 artillery pieces back to Louie's private living quarters. It was dark. Over in a big wicker chair, wrapped up in a blanket, was Rudy. "Rudy?" I started to say, "The general's looking for you," but he interrupted.

"I'm in big trouble," he said after a long pause, a grunt and a moan. "I got a disease."

"What?" I still couldn't take it in.

"Just got back from R and R in Bangkok and I've got something. My testicles are swelled up the size of oranges and I'm really in pain. I got to get help. I can't . . ." and he stopped short. "Can you help me?"

Somehow, what he was talking about just didn't register, and I must have stammered, "I don't understand." Louie whispered, "Damn, Chappie, he's got the clap—got to have some penicillin."

"The clap. VD?" I must have looked pretty startled, as Louie grinned, something he almost never did. It took another few seconds to finally sink in.

"OK, wait here."

I walked to the doc's tent and explained the situation. The doc busted out laughing. He was a Southern Baptist from Alabama and laughed all the way back to Louie's tent. I tried to explain the seriousness of the situation: with Rudy being a priest, his getting VD was not going to go over well. And to make matters worse, the general was hot on his trail.

I was pretty impressed with the doc. When we got back to Louie's tent, he showed all the empathy and bedside manner that he could. He questioned Rudy a little, didn't make any judgment, and gave him a gigantic shot of penicillin.

"How long before this works?" I asked.

"Well, pretty fast, but it's going to take three days for him to be able to move around easily."

I thought, *How can we hide him for three days? The general is already looking for him and it's only a matter of time.*

The next time the general's aide called I said, "Well Colonel, Father Rudy is pretty sick. He has the runs and we can't get him out of the field yet. Too dangerous. Maybe tomorrow."

"How did he get way out there?"

"You mean literally?"

"You know what I mean, Captain."

When they called you Captain as opposed to Chaplain, you knew you were in trouble.

"Well, it was my fault."

"The general is not going to like this."

Well, the general didn't like lots of things. I didn't know the general, but he was a one-star, worse than most and considered Rudy to be his personal chaplain. I had heard he could be brutal. Rudy was always complaining about him. But the general wanted him to say mass every day. Great! I concocted a story about Rudy saying mass for some GIs on bridge duty and then getting sick and not being able to get back to headquarters. The bridge was actually more like a little footpath, but it went across to a little spit that was barely above water. Once you got over the little footpath, it spread out in several directions and was a valuable piece of real estate—made good hiding places for the VC.

When high tide flooded in, it was impossible to get to, and when the tide ebbed, just the small footpath was usable, and many VC or NVA camped out and went back and forth. At least one chopper had been shot down trying to access the small landing zone on the little strip of ground. This was dangerous duty. The men guarding the bridge wanted mass, and it was my job to support them. The men didn't know they needed mass, I'm not even sure if they were Catholic, but they definitely needed mass.

What I was actually giving the general, not even realizing it at the time, was a justification for military chaplains. The Constitution guaranteed that even though men were at war, the country shouldn't fail to provide some semblance of the religion they would have had if they had not been called to war. It sounded good. Also, it fit in well with the unofficial word we had after the Tet offensive:

thousands of NVA soldiers were trapped between the city of Hue and the South China Sea. We were hunting them and this bridge was a conduit. It sounded good to me.

The general threatened to send his helicopter after Rudy but the danger of it must have outweighed his desire. Lucky for us. *You're coming in broken and distorted.*

*Ideals are like stars; you will not succeed in touching them with your hands.*
*But like the seafaring man on the desert of waters, you choose them as your guides and following them you will reach your destiny.*

CARL SCHURZ

# Hold That Tiger

(A "tiger" is a night ambush.)

*Three fourths of the four-man fire team moved as slow as molasses toward the captain. One peeled off to relieve himself while the other two wearily snaked over to where the young commander sat.*

*"I hate this roaming 'round at night chasing after little men in black pajamas," said a bored-looking Puerto Rican named Hector from the Bronx.*

*"Watch your back," one of his buddies called out, kind of a word of encouragement.*

*Mostly said as shorthand for "Thank God it ain't my turn for a tiger tonight."*

*"Hell, man, I'm doing that all my life. What's different about Nam?"*

*The other GI was a small kid from Clear Lake, Iowa, named Luke—looked like someone who would wait on you at Sears or be more at home in a chemistry lab. The captain spoke: "Set up your ambush along here." He pointed to a little trail leading into the ville. "Go to the east of the road instead of west at the clearing. See here," he seemed to say to the air as his audience engaged in the thousand-yard stare. They were to form a triangle and wait. "Got your claymores?"*

*They nodded.*

FROM THE BOOK *FREE FIRE ZONE*

Fear was the great equalizer in Vietnam. I'm sure soldiers in any war can attest to the same emotions—indescribable—a kind of overwhelming palpable inability to know your name, where you are or what you are supposed to be doing. Chaplains were not immune to it. Fear affected all of us differently.

I wish I had been a little more mature about handling it. This could be said about plenty of things, but especially about fear. I always viewed it as anxiety, but it was something more. In a firefight, when the bullets started flying, I would forget my name, where I was, everything. I actually have seen some men so overcome by fear that they could not budge. I always thought of Sergeant Henry. For most, it became part of their existence, and when shooting started, they simply did what they had to do. What I hated worse than anything was the plop, plop of mortar rounds. It is a sound like you can't imagine. When you hear them, you know they're coming after you. And, I'd be hoping, "Please dear Lord, let somebody call in artillery or gunships or something." When it's over, there's a rush of feelings: thankfulness and "Did I measure up?"

In Vietnam, as in all wars, the saddest times of all were the holidays—men were away from their families, thinking about all the holiday activities back home. Much of it was probably fantasized, but this didn't make any difference— most things are when one is away from home. When the men had been back home and the activities were actually going on, they might consider them an enormous hassle, but at war you would never admit such blasphemy—those times back home were cherished memories.

We had a devastating tragedy just before Christmas — talk about making us sad and mad. A chopper was bringing the Christmas mail to us in a giant sling underneath its body. The sling was an enclosed contraption that enabled the bird to bring more supplies than it could carry inside, and it was literally swinging under the helicopter. It most likely held some other things as well, ammo and the like, but the precious part of the cargo was all the Christmas mail and packages from home. We were anticipating it eagerly.

Somewhere along the way from Sally to the FSB, the chopper hit some turbulence and dropped the sling.

Before they could get down and retrieve the mail, the Vietnamese had gotten to it and were nowhere to be found. They could have been enemy but more than likely were friendlies. Regardless of who they were, it was a very tough situation, and had the troops been able to get to the ville of the people who stole our mail, another My Lai might have been in the offing.

*Forgiveness is the windblown bud*
*which blooms in placid beauty at Verdun.*
*Forgiveness is the tiny slate-gray sparrow*
*which has built its nest of twigs and string among the*
*shards of glass upon the wall of shame.*
*Forgiveness is the child who laughs in merry ecstasy*
*beneath the toothed fence that closes in DaNang.*
*Forgiveness is the fragrance of the violet*
*which still clings fast to the heel that crushed it.*
*Forgiveness is the broken dream*
*which hides itself within the corner of the mind oft called forgetfulness,*
*so that it will not bring pain to the dreamer.*
*Forgiveness is the reed which stands up straight and green*
*when nature's mighty rampage halts, full spent.*
*Forgiveness is a God who will not leave us after all we've done.*

GEORGE ROEMISCH

# You Are Not Mad
# with Me Have You?

(a nonsensical expression to take the edge off a tense situation)

I basically blew off any worries about the general who was looking for Rudy. I had a job to do regardless of anybody's views. I was told that this general saw me out with one of the companies and was apoplectic. I remember him asking

219

the company commander: "What is the chaplain doing out here? He's going to get killed. This is no place for him." He went on and on. Later the company commander said to me, "Chaplain, this guy's got a hard-on for you. What did you do to piss him off?" He must have really complained and thrown his weight around. The word came down from somewhere that I was not to be in the field.

I couldn't understand why somebody was not telling the general to take a flying leap. He was not even in my chain of command. Maybe I overestimated my own importance. I figured I'd get out tomorrow and let things cool off. I remember the incident with incredible clarity because I was with Delta Company and the contact was heavy—artillery and gunships and "jolly green giants" everywhere (C-47 cargo planes that, among many things, dropped a lot of flares). We got hit from every direction with mortars, small arms fire, and even some RPGs (rocket-propelled grenades). The fight went on most of the night. We had several guys hit and could not get the dustoffs in.

I hated the nights. The obvious reason was that crawling around, trying to help with the wounded, I couldn't see. Always, as dark started to close in on us, regardless of where I might be, everybody's mood turned somber. It seemed like everything happened at night. The night belonged to the enemy.

As abruptly as all the action had started, it stopped, as most firefights did.

As morning light broke, I knew it was going to be a long day. We had at least five dead and several wounded.

I walked around to where all the dead were, prayed, and did my ritual—made sure that each man was covered with his poncho liner. Occasional rounds kept coming in; probably snipers way off in the distance just messing with us. But nobody took chances.

We needed to move, but we would not leave our dead, plus we had two badly wounded and some with less serious injuries. Fighting had erupted about 10 clicks (kilometers) to the north and the battalion commander wanted Delta to move toward them, as a suspected NVA unit had lit up one of the companies. I suggested to the CO that he leave a couple of guys with me and go. Our AO wasn't very vulnerable from the rear, so there was little chance of problems. We'd wait for the dustoffs and then hump on over.

Finally the dustoffs came for the wounded and dead. This was always hard and sad—guys had a tough time when fellow GIs bought the farm. I did what I could, but was not much comfort. The best thing was to get back to business as usual. No time to grieve or sort things out. I'd do my ritual and move on.

For every dead GI, I have a memory. One, for instance, had gotten a "Dear John" letter from his girlfriend. It wouldn't have been so bad, but one of his best buddies was the "Jody" (the culprit who had stolen his girl). As we talked, I discovered that he was not all torn up; he was just angry that his buddy did the deed. Finally, he admitted that maybe if the tables had been reversed, he might have done the same thing. We'd planned to talk about it later, but later never came.

*God is our refuge and strength,*
*always ready to help in times of trouble.*
*So be not afraid, even if the earth is shaken*
*and mountains fall into the ocean depths.*
*The Lord Almighty is with us,*
*He is our refuge.*

PSALMS 46

# Going on to Montana

My favorite TV miniseries ever was *Lonesome Dove*. The story is about cowboys driving a herd of cattle from Texas to Montana. Along the way, various tragedies occur and death is often one of them. Gus, played by Robert Duvall, was a renaissance man. When someone died, they always had a small service or someone said a word or two at the burial and then the concept was, "Let's the rest of us go on to Montana."

This is how it was in Vietnam. At times, I got a chance to say a word, but mostly, we went "on to Montana." We didn't really grieve. The trauma of ungrieved deaths usually rears its ugly head somehow, often years later in the form of what we now call PTSD (post-traumatic stress disorder). Combat takes a toll, especially on youngsters, and because of their macho ways, the toll might not be readily apparent when it is happening.

I kept up with lots of guys after Vietnam—many who were with me in Nam later were withdrawn, angry; alternately involved and detached. Many vets are overwhelmed with guilt and have recurring nightmares. There are times when I wake up in a cold sweat, reliving with amazing clarity specific situations in Vietnam, and this is 38 years after the event. If someone like me—who has attempted tenaciously to understand himself and has the help of education and experience—has difficulties, what can we say for those who try to continue their lives without this help? The sadness is realizing that many vets are still unable to move on emotionally and have lost the most productive years of their lives.

## Is PTSD Real?

Post-traumatic stress disorder (PTSD) has entered the American lexicon on a wholesale scale only since the Vietnam war. It isn't some designer pop malady come to light through a head-in-the-clouds therapist but something very, very real. Most combat Vietnam vets have varying degrees of PTSD. It makes sense, if you think about it. Here's a guy in combat for a year. Almost every day he's at risk, scared witless, killing or being killed, losing his buddies.

The statistics bear it out: on average Vietnam veterans spent almost two hundred days in combat, facing the rigors of risk, uncertainty, and seeing buddies killed. A combat soldier in Vietnam bonded to his fellow soldiers in an unusual way because of operating for days, weeks, and months in small groups. During what slack time he had, he sat around and shared experiences with a small group of buddies: loves, life, photos. And then all of a sudden the friends, the confidants were gone—they bit the dust, bought the farm; their presence and camaraderie were forever lost.

Now, to make matters worse, if a soldier survived his combat time, his government provided no reentry program. One day he was in the jungle with all of its dangers, living a lifestyle of fright, machismo, resignation, great highs and lows; then, with lightning speed, he was back on the streets of Detroit, expected to resume his life like he'd been off to summer camp.

For the doubters, let me boil it down to practical terms. You and your wife and family have just come from church, and you're heading to Grandma's house for lunch. On the way, you witness a terrible automobile accident. People are killed, bodies litter the highway, there's blood and gore; you instinctively jump out and help. You attempt to stop the bleeding and apply all your Red Cross training. You witness moaning, dying, screaming, and moments of hell. Mercifully, it ends. You continue on to Grandma's as though nothing happened; there's no effect, no problem, you don't even share the stories, the tales, the experience; after all, you do not want to interfere with the life and enjoyment of others. And, instinctively you feel that they don't want to know about it anyway. You and your experience of the accident and the aftermath are a microcosm of the Vietnam combat veteran's return to society.

My nemesis, the general who wanted me out of the field, launched a crusade to get me out that seemed to take on a life of its own. The battalion executive officer and the battalion commander mentioned that I probably was going to be transferred. Both of them seemed to want to talk about it. I got the feeling they wanted me to provide some sort of fuel to help prevent it from happening, but I didn't know what. The battalion commander pulled me aside and said that it might be for the best. I'd paid my dues. He was stumbling for words and mentioned the sapper attack of a few days earlier. He didn't come right out and ask me if I knew any details, but he left it open. I never responded.

The entire issue of my leaving the field was OBE (overcome by events). The company CO came by, smiled, and said, "Chaplain, don't guess you need to get out of the field. The general who wanted you gone got killed last night." What! Then it became a joke: "If you mess with the chaplain, God will get you." I felt bad about the general, whom I didn't even know.

Somewhere down the road, however, the decision was made that I should move to a safer unit—aviation or something around Camp Eagle. The problem, according to the powers that be, was that the morale issue was serious. If I were killed, it would so deflate the troops that it had to be avoided. We had been over this before, and I was tired of it.

Moving me didn't make sense in this environment anyway. A person could get killed anywhere. Front lines were nonexistent; the entire country was a war zone. It didn't seem like good logic to me, and it went against my personal credo. I think the idea of taking an aggressive approach is all the same whether you're talking about life or war. If you sit back worrying about it, you still might buy the farm. Get out there and live and fight and let the time pass. *Do some good!* I feel the same way about the issue of terrorism in our country. We can't stop living. We have to protect ourselves the best we can and not worry about it.

I put up such a fight about being moved that finally somebody, somewhere relented. I think it might have been because my replacement was in a near-catatonic state. I felt really bad for him—he had already been to the field once and was so terrified that he became a burden to the unit. They sent him down south for a while and now wanted to give him another chance. I understood. Later on, I saw him at Sally—where things seemed much safer. He was doing a great job.

The point is that fear affects us all differently. Some can't function, others function pretty well, and there are some who seem to ignore it. I seem to be in the last category. Why? I think it has to do with spatial memory—a lack of short-term memory or one that is not readily available to call up recent events. For instance, if something happened yesterday, it doesn't seem to dramatically impact today.

Focusing is no small thing for those of us with ADD. In combat, a firefight happens when it happens, and the fear of previous ones didn't seem to make me dread that which had not happened yet.

I do believe, in retrospect, that I am ADD. The joke I make all the time has to do with my generation. As a youngster growing up in North Carolina, when I couldn't be still or was disruptive, the teacher would come by and slap me upside the head. A few of those and she had my attention.

Our world has changed, obviously, and we no longer take such stringent approaches to disruptive kids. The thing that is now a bother to me quite possibly saved my life in Vietnam. With ADD, one revels in new experiences and excitement, going from one thing to the other. Somehow, that helped me through the war.

*I expect to pass through this world but once.*
*Any good therefore that I can do,*
*or any kindness that I can show*
*to any fellow creature, let me do it now.*
*Let me not defer or neglect it,*
*for I shall not pass this way again.*

WILLIAM PENN

# Off We Go
# into the Wild Blue Yonder

I almost was killed three times in Vietnam. One was the experience with the recon platoon. The second was an event that, to this day, I think about with awe. We had a little beach area called Coco Beach. It was a great little stretch of beach that reminded me of the beaches I came to know in California: Carmel, Ocean Beach in San Francisco, or Stinson or Muir Beach in Marin County. Maybe even Daytona. In my mind's eye, I could see driving my brother's '57 Chevy convertible right on the beach at Coco in the Nam.

This particular operation belonged to the Navy, as they stored JP-4 jet fuel there, and compared with the Army, they lived the good life. While we were providing security for them at Coco, they supported us by letting us eat in the chow hall and enjoy some of their goodies. This setup was not without a few conflicts, but for the most part, it was much better than what we were used to. Throughout my time in Nam, this was a place of many experiences.

Coco was usually used for companies or platoons that had been hit hard, had lost a lot of troops, and needed to have a break and get resupplied—with both goods and men. It provided a bit of healing at war. I'd go down there, have services, and spend time with the troops—a good experience as a rule. Once I was at Coco when a large troupe of singers/entertainers was around. I saw parts of the show; beaucoup beautiful girls. I noticed that most of the guys seemed to be at the mess hall end of the beach, where the entertainment was. It made sense—these were young guys and there were girls. For some reason, late one afternoon I walked down in that direction, and I saw a line snaking way out from the back of the mess hall toward me. I asked a couple of guys what they were doing. "Oh just getting some autographs." Boy, was I was naïve.

They were autographs all right—very personal autographs! The upshot: almost the entire company had to stand down because of VD. One of the guys told me about it: classic gonorrhea, three or four days and the gift that keeps on giving.

One day I arrived at the beach after services at Mongoose, stayed most of the day, and wanted to get back to the FSB. Ordinarily I would have had a vehicle, but I didn't and was catching a ride on a chopper. It was bound for Eagle but would drop me off on the way. I was good to go.

The helicopter came in at dusk and a familiar thought hit me as I hopped aboard: *Hope we don't get shot out of the air.* I never really worried about it. Helicopters had become a way of life. The Huey, sometimes called a "slick," was the workhorse of Nam. On board were three enlisted guys including an E7 (sergeant first class). They weren't my guys, but that was not unusual, as we weren't the only troops who came to Coco. They were probably heading to Eagle after they dropped me off, which was about a five- or ten-minute jaunt at most. We lifted off and headed out over the South China sea. It was beautiful. The water was as blue as any sky I'd ever seen. *If the Vietnamese could only get their stuff together—what they ought to do is quit this fighting and develop these beaches and the tourists would flock in and life would be great.*

We flew along the coast for what seemed like 30 minutes, and I thought, *I should have been at Mongoose 15 minutes ago.* I started to say something, but then figured maybe they were going to Eagle first and then dropping me off. I had learned that you did what you were told or went along and it worked out. These young helicopter pilots were great. I was often amazed at their youthful appearance; more likely than not, they weren't even old enough to drink. In fact, the Army had gotten so short of pilots that they had a program in which eighteen-year-olds could become warrant officers and helicopter pilots. Think about it: an eighteen-year-old driving one of these machines at war—daredevil and extreme sports personified. Many lost their lives—more than should have. I knew several well and appreciated their efforts. Some of their deaths could be attributed to commanders who put their lives needlessly into risky situations—an egotistical commander, battalion or brigade, or general, trying to be a hero.

I remember one case where a commander wanted to fly in thick fog (which often formed in early morning and late evening). He saw himself as John Wayne and ordered the pilot to fly to a place in the mountains where the enemy had been spotted. The only way the pilot could do it was to go to the edge of the mountain and snake his way up it, but by doing this he exposed himself to enemy fire. The ship was unbelievably vulnerable, and the worst happened. The VC, with little trouble, shot the aircraft out of the sky, killing them all. This could have been avoided and it made me incredibly angry.

At times, pilots would take amazing chances for the troops, taking in ammo under dangerous circumstances,

> **HOW SHALL WE DIE?**
> *So live that when thy summons comes to join that innumerable caravan which moves to that mysterious realm where each shall take his chamber in the silent halls of death. Go not like the quarry slave at night, scourged to his dungeon, but sustained and soothed by an unfaltering trust, approach thy grave like one who wraps the drapery of his couch about him and lies down to pleasant dreams.*
>
> WILLIAM CULLEN BRYANT

usually in heavy action. Huey pilots would use their aircraft as dustoff choppers to get the wounded out in the midst of withering fire. Helicopter pilots were unbelievably brave in the Nam. Real heroes!

But now, in the helicopter that should have been taking me to Mongoose, it was not just dark, it was black. I was getting more than a little apprehensive. We were still skimming along the water, and we'd been out close to an hour. *What was going on?* I leaned forward and motioned to one of the pilots, who shook his head. It was now too dark to see the other troops, but the NCO whispered to me, "Chaplain, what's going on?"

"I don't know."

We waited in silence. Then one of the pilots handed me a headset and said, "Chaplain, we are lost over the sea."

I could not believe what I was hearing. We kept flying, and I wondered what we were going to do and pondered what the possibilities might be. I was as calm as a cucumber. The headset came on and the copilot said, "Chaplain, we are just about out of fuel and are going to ditch in the sea. Tell the others."

I prayed and thought, *Lord, I hate this and I'm going to miss seeing Meg grow up and Jackie. I was a pretty sorry husband.* But I was still not frightened and motioned for the NCO to come closer and actually pulled him toward me. I was convinced that we were all going to die and felt bad for the rest of the men with me. The fear was breathable. Time seemed suspended. I started to shout to the NCO and the others that they should prepare to hit the water.

Suddenly, the helicopter popped over land. I discovered later that we were 50 miles south of where we should have been. I was so grateful to be alive—for all of us—that I didn't even question how it happened. Was this a miracle? I'm reluctant to talk about such things happening as miracles. Many miracles happened in the Nam and there were events that could have used a miracle but it didn't happen.

I've often pondered about the meaning of this experience. I think that when you are convinced you are going to die—however you accept it—the fear of death ceases to have the same meaning ever again. In some ways, such an experience makes one almost immune from the fear of death.

Through the years, when I have discussed faith as related to death, I often talk about it in philosophical terms: *This life is only a temporary place; it is a matter of transition from this life into the next.* I believe it! This world is not my home!

*As a man grows older, he values the voice of
experience more and the voice of prophecy less.
He finds more of life's wealth in the common
pleasures—home, health and children.
He thinks more about the work of men and less
about their wealth. He begins to appreciate his
own father a little more. He hurries less, and
usually makes more progress. He esteems the
friendship of God a little more highly.*

ROY L. SMITH

# Leaning Forward into the Battle Zone

Sometimes I'd have six or eight services on a Sunday and a dozen or so in a week's time. Every time we slowed down, I'd say, "Let's have a church service," or so it seemed. If the troops didn't like it, they never let on. Once, when the priest was with me, in the middle of the mass we got mortared, and then a lone sniper popped off a round or two. Of course, our troops opened up, firing back big-time.

At the Fire Support Base on Sundays, I'd go from tent to tent and kick guys out for services. Usually, I'd say, "This is what your mom expects of me." We'd fill up the tent.

The services were short and sweet. Most of the time, the music came from a little tape recorder and we always sang "Amazing Grace," "He Leadeth Me," and "Blessed Assurance." It was fun. For the life of me, I cannot remember a single one of my sermons. But I know I had them—I always tried to be upbeat, provide some inspiration, and let the troops know that the war would end. I had a great battalion commander for a short period who loved to sing and actually led the music for awhile. He said one Sunday morning, "Chaplain, this is the worst singing I've ever heard."

So I said, "I know—why don't you help us out?" I never expected him to, but he did. The battalion surgeon chewed me out once for having a big knife hanging from my belt. It actually wasn't even mine but one of the troops insisted that I keep it for him. I took it off afterwards. Thanks Doc.

Soldiers in combat reminded me a little of athletes when it came to superstitions. They'd have premonitions of their deaths. I'd assure them that they were not going to die and just because a dream or a thought or something sinister became imbedded temporarily in their psyche didn't mean it was going to happen.

They were always giving me things or asking me to hold something for them until they got out of the field. Sometimes it was a tangible way for them to say, *Thanks, and if something happens to me, I want you to have this*—it could be anything: cookies from home, captured weapons; anything to show affection and to show that at a future date they would reclaim it. I accepted them graciously and usually said, "It's like putting this [whatever it might be— weapon, knife, picture, trinket] in the Bank of America." It made troops smile and feel assured.

On more occasions than I like to remember, they didn't claim them because they'd been killed. It was sad beyond belief. If I could, I contacted the parents or next of kin and sent the item to them or described it. For some, it opened up an additional wound, so I had to be cautious.

Once a young troop gave me some trinkets—little carved figures—he'd gotten from some kids in a ville they swept through. The family treasured them as the last tangible evidence of their son and his existence. Until I left Vietnam, that family sent a steady stream of goodies for the troops: cookies, books, cases of Kool-Aid and the prized Tabasco sauce. This probably helped their grieving. Even amidst the pain, it was satisfying to be a chaplain at war—to be helping.

One of the troops did get me in a jam. Because we were often in a free-fire zone, lots of things were simply lying around. Buddhas were especially treasured, mostly because they were ornate. If a company was sweeping through a ville, more than likely they saw hundreds of small Buddhas—they were so commonplace. One soldier had picked up a really nice elaborate one with all the spiritual truths represented by multiple pairs of raised hands. He said, "Chaplain, I'd really like to keep this." I would have objected, but the village was already on fire from being prepped by artillery, so the Buddha was probably going to be destroyed anyway. So I said, *OK, what the hay!* What I didn't know was that on that very morning, the commanding general had issued an edict that we were not to take any more souvenirs. My chopper landed, and as I was getting off it with a gigantic Buddha in my arms, there were the battalion and brigade commanders getting on.

*I will lift up my eyes to the hills*
*from whence cometh my help.*
*My help comes from God.*
PSALMS 121:1–2

# Living in the Twilight Zone

I was living in mortal danger another time and don't think I even knew it. A captain in my unit wanted to get married. In Vietnam, the Army made it very difficult to marry locals—time was the factor. It took forever to prepare the paperwork, and by the time it was ready, the GI was ready to go home or had already gone. This Army policy probably saved many young soldiers from doing something that they would more than likely regret.

The captain had extended his stay to get the paperwork finished. He was a good-looking West Pointer; she, supposedly, was a Vietnamese university professor. I was skeptical, mainly because many of the GIs, especially those in the south, would say their girlfriends were from the university when in fact, they met them in a bar. (Maybe the University of Life, I thought, and I don't mean to disparage the girls—they did what they needed to do to survive.)

In the captain's case, I discovered that the woman was, in fact, a university professor. I didn't know the captain well. He was a company commander before I arrived and then was moved to brigade headquarters. He asked me if I could perform the wedding. Like many future events, it was a long way off—at least a few months, and in Nam, a month is a lifetime. "Sure," I said.

The time arrived for the wedding. I was supposed to be in charge of the religious part of the ceremony, which was mostly a symbolic gesture. The embassy did the official part, but it seemed to be important to him for me to be involved—it legitimized their relationship. I had to go to Phan Thiet, which was, as I understood it, a university town and cultural center.

Well, in a half-assed way, as my dad would say, I didn't make any preparations and left out of the field to go to Bien Hoa and then on to Phan Thiet. We were in beaucoup contact and I hated to leave my unit, but a promise is a promise.

I was supposed to meet the captain at the MacV compound. I got lost and was wandering around the town, which seemed pretty calm and larger than I had thought. A jeep pulled up beside me and an American demanded that I get into his vehicle. I almost didn't, but the alternative was to keep walking around in a fog—or as we would say in North Carolina, like a chicken with its head cut off.

The guy turned out to be a civilian CIA type. After I told him who I was and where I was attempting to go, he told me I was in a hotbed of VC activities and needed to be off the streets *now!* Whatever was happening was about to go down. He took me to the MacV compound and I spent the night. True to his predictions, all hell broke loose—kind of a mini Tet offensive, somebody explained to me.

The compound was like a walled-in fortress. It had once been a Buddhist seminary, and there was a courtyard with little rooms off it. When there were no students, it became a government building and then the headquarters for a Special Forces A team and MacV. There was a big door that opened into the courtyard from outside. Sometime during the night, it got blown out by an RPG. All night long there was firing, and helicopter gunships blasted away somewhere close by. I remember thinking, *I hope that I haven't come to this place to get zapped. I could have gotten it at home.* (Home being my battalion.) I didn't sleep a wink, and by daylight it was quiet. *Just another night in paradise.*

The next morning, my one-time savior arranged for a helicopter to take me to Bien Hoa. He was really a nice guy and told me that when he picked me up I had been within a hair of being captured by the VC. His sources said the VC had been stalking me for 30 minutes and were closing in. He was, in fact, surprised that when they saw him intervene they didn't kill both of us.

• • •

Being in Vietnam was a surreal existence no matter how you look at it. I recently saw the newer version of *Apocalypse Now*. It was amazing 30 years afterwards to view this satire, this parody of Vietnam—and I found it more believable now. When it was happening to you, you didn't see it this way. It was real, and in a sense, it was the only thing that was real. The shared experience will always remain with Vietnam veterans.

Not long ago, I was on the freeway and passed an old beat-up truck with a South Vietnamese flag on it and a bumper sticker that said, "I was at Chu Chi." I gave him a salute. We were from different worlds. Our lives may have taken entirely different turns, but we were brothers.

I've always thought that if Vietnam veterans could get organized, we could make an enormous impact on the country. We are not all the same and don't share the same views, but get us talking about Nam and we are there—we share so many experiences. I wish I knew where many of my buddies whose lives I shared are today. Maybe this camaraderie exists because we fought a war in Vietnam and we fought a war at home and both wars scarred us.

I never did get to the captain's wedding.

*Our God and soldier we alike adore,*
*When at the break of ruin, not before,*
*After deliverance, both alike requited,*
*Our God forgotten, and our soldiers slighted.*

FRANCES QUARLES (1592–1644)

# This Could Be a Sitcom
# If It Wasn't So Sad

I never once stopped at Phu Bai that I didn't think of my buddy Father Bertrand (not his real name)—Bernie, we called him. He and I were in the Basic Chaplain's Course in Brooklyn. I remember him for many reasons, but one in particular—he didn't take any of it seriously. We'd have instructors talking about heavy-duty issues, and he'd make a joke. He called it the "basic praying and Bible-reading course." I had heard he was at the field hospital in Phu Bai and had tried to find him several times, but to no avail. Everybody knew him but he was like Howard Hughes—

everybody had heard of him but no one had seen him. (They sometimes said the same thing about me.)

I had gone to visit some of my troops who'd been hit, and on the way out, I asked a nurse if she knew Father Bernie. She turned ashen and was visibly shaken. *What was this?* She started to say something and stopped. The situation was momentarily very uncomfortable. We didn't see many "round eyes" as we called them, and talking to the nurses or Red Cross donut dollies was a nice distraction—a little harmless flirting. *What was going on?*

*What sacrifices nurses in Nam made! I admire them to this day more than any other professionals I know. In Vietnam, the nurses didn't have a clue as to what they were getting into any more than the rest of us did, but it was somewhat different with them. What little recognition they've gotten, like China Beach on TV, has been very right on. They were dedicated and held many a young soldier's hand as he died because Mom wasn't available. Think ER on TV. Every day it was ER and worse—and real!*

I went outside the ward, which was in a Quonset hut whose rounded shape supposedly made it enemy-proof. I doubt it. The nurse came out, looked at her feet a little and finally said,

"You're a chaplain, right?"

"Yes, you got it."

"I've seen you here before, visiting soldiers."

I nodded. We didn't say anything for a moment. I was uncomfortable. I hadn't been to that class yet where they teach you it's OK to be silent.

Finally, she said, "Could I talk to you in private?"

"Sure."

"Is it confidential?"

"Sure." I quickly ran over possibilities in my mind. *What could it be? Personal problem, CO (conscientious objector), what?* Like most of the helping professionals in Vietnam, or anywhere else for that matter, chaplains think they've heard it all. The truth is, we haven't. But with experience, our senses become more finely tuned—we hear a few words and can tell what the problem is long before the person has spilled the story.

"When can I see you?"

"Well, what about now?"

We walked over toward the little canteen. In the distance, I noticed another person looking at us. As we got closer, I could see that it was Father Bernie. I could hardly believe my eyes and spontaneously ran and hugged him. I pumped his hand and said, "Wow, Bernie, where have you been? I know there's no Brooklyn or pasta or New York theater." I was so happy to see him!

He was equally happy to see me too, I could tell. We started jabbering, and suddenly I remembered the nurse. She was gone.

"Oh, no," I said, "I was talking to this pretty nurse and then saw you. Now she's gone." We chatted and caught up. He'd been in Nam for nine months. At that time, I had been in about three. We discussed the war—how crazy it was, what we'd been doing, the good times in New York. It was so good to see him. Bernie was generous, and when we'd been together in New York, he'd taught me all the little things that only New Yorkers know—like that uptown always means north, downtown, south.

I forgot all about the nurse and went back to the unit with a promise to check back later. I came about every week or so depending on the action. Sure enough, I saw Bernie with regularity. It was always great and I felt good about his being there and knew his ministry was the very best for soldiers. He told me he was trying to extend, but his bishop wouldn't let him.

"What? Are you nuts? Get the hell out of here and get home."

Then he dropped the bombshell. He had fallen in love with a nurse. He didn't know what to do and wanted to stay and sort it out. And, to make it worse, she was married.

"What a mess," he sighed and looked about as forlorn as anybody I'd ever seen. I was 28 years old—what did I know? Nothing. It was 1968, the dark ages compared to now.

"Wow, Bernie. What are you going to do?" I'd had counseling classes but didn't know what to say—I only knew I should listen, which was not all that bad for starters.

"I don't know how I can live without her," he said. "I've never felt like this, really. My family will be disgraced. What about her own family? She has two children. It's a no-win situation."

*Bernie,* I thought, *you're answering your own questions.* Bertrand was one of a dozen or so children in a big Irish family where the greatest honor was to have a priest or a nun in the family—to give to the church one of your own. I felt so helpless and felt his pain.

He left for home. I saw him just before he departed for the south. The same nurse who wanted to talk with me saw him off. I finally got it. Later on, I ran into her. I didn't say anything and neither did she.

If nothing else, war taught me an unusual tolerance. It isn't always right or wrong—rules and regulations; often, it's gray and then more gray. Even with my lack of knowledge, I understood that things like this happened. They take place at war and it's no movie.

Bernie was a kind, considerate human being surrounded by the tragedies of war. He met someone. They clicked and clung to each other amid the tragedies of life and death. He later became an archbishop and I heard from him for a long time. He told me that he and his friend had talked a few times but agreed that theirs had been a war relationship and now the war was over.

*Pain that cannot forget*
*falls like tears on our hearts*
UNKNOWN

# Were You Always a Chaplain?

M any soldiers in Vietnam who still had time on their military obligation after the war went to places like Germany and were expected to be regular soldiers. Think about it: at war everyday, life on the line; suddenly, they have to worry about formations, inspections—many simply crashed and burned emotionally and sometimes physically. I blame the military—those making the decisions at the highest levels—for not recognizing how important it was for troops to have a reentry program. The Pentagon bureaucrats were the first in a long line of those denigrating the Vietnam vet.

Vietnam vets showed up in places like Germany scarred and damaged. I was in Germany for part of that time. I would see these young soldiers with a year or two left in the military—as the military called it, at "their next duty station." They simply couldn't put Vietnam behind them. How could they be expected to? During the moment between their war life and their real life, somewhat like being suspended in time, they drank, smoked dope, anything to get some relief. They didn't have to worry about anybody shooting at them. Consequently, they dropped further into the abyss. All the pent-up emotions they couldn't share came to the surface masked sometimes by unfortunate behavior.

Yesterday they'd been out on patrol or sitting by a trail, waiting for "Charles," and now they were in Germany, saying, "Ein Bier, bitte." Probably, before they came to Germany, they'd gone on leave to the States. They'd visited family who didn't want to hear their war stories or see their pictures. Why should they? They'd been viewing it on TV for years.

And the families couldn't help but notice the changes in their sons. Johnny came marching home, but Johnny was not the same Johnny. Images burned into Johnny's mind—grass houses afire, women and black-eyed kids staring at big GIs trudging through their villes.

I think that's why a movie like *Platoon* made an impact. I remember sitting in a theater in San Francisco watching it, hoping I wouldn't like it. It was an ordeal to sit there, but upon reflection, I realize that it was one soldier's depiction of his time in hell/Vietnam. To make a story out of it, Hollywood made some things up, but the general idea of how it went down was pretty good.

Returning GIs probably had no idea of the view of the war held by Americans who cared. And of course, not all cared. Those who did were the moms and dads and girlfriends and occasionally classmates of soldiers.

Most who had any contact with returning GIs wanted them to "move on," whatever that was. Those who made it through Nam often didn't make it through life.

It has been said that the military chaplaincy ruins you for the civilian clergy. Maybe I'm the one who said it. What does being a chaplain in Vietnam do to you? How could being at war not shape one's view of life, and in the case of the chaplain, shape one's ministry? Maybe those who enter the military chaplaincy are a little or a lot odd—maybe they didn't fit in all that well anyway. Maybe they were looking for their "place at the table" and found it in the Nam. Perhaps!

What Vietnam brought out maybe more than anything was the ministry of presence. On occasion, among ourselves, we joked about it, but it was real. There was something about the chaplain being present in the face of danger with those who endured it constantly that made a difference. It was the shared experience, but it was more: a trooper—a line doggie, a grunt—*had* to be there. As a young trooper told me early on, "Chaplain, what makes you different and special is that you don't *have* to be here."

When I finally left Vietnam, I didn't feel special, but I sure felt different. I was a completely different man than the cherry lieutenant who had boarded that cargo plane a year before. I was a man of peace who tried to remind brave warriors about the Prince of Peace. I hope I helped them. I know I will never forget them.

# Epilogue (Observations)

After I retired from the military, I took the first year and put together a tribute to my hometown hero, General William C. Lee, the father of the American airborne. Then I became pastor of a great little church, an hour and a half north of San Francisco in the wonderful community of Rio Vista in California's Delta country. Rio Vista means a "river view," as the town is at the mouth of the Sacramento River.

I was there for eight years. I can still hardly believe it. I meant to stay two or three years, but things kept happening: 9/11, then the Iraq war started, and I always need a project to somehow express myself. The folks in Rio Vista were wonderful because as part of my expression, I did a little weekly newsletter and could never resist inserting my opinions. I tried to be evenhanded, but I'm sure there were times I must have come across as leaning one way or the other. When I retired from the church, I had several things I wanted to do before I "slept," and the Airborne Press webzine gave me the chance to do them.

I've always been a writer, and I could easily cover my walls with rejection slips. The wonderful thing about the Internet is that it gives people like myself a chance to express their thoughts, regardless of whether they are read. Once I've written something, it's done and I'm on to the next thing.

Of course, the war continues to rage in Iraq—into its third year with no end in sight. The war pains me immensely and almost renders me useless at times; writing about it has been my salvation in a sense. It is not in me *not* to comment on the war. Throughout my ministry, I have been guided by the idea of comforting the afflicted, but also afflicting the comfortable, and there's not much chance that I'll change. A commander once told me, "Chaplain, your job always is to make the Army a better place." This became my goal, and it was not without some trouble that I tried to achieve it. I was "fired" four times in my career—twice for running my mouth and twice more for refusing to back down in my quest to make the Army a better place. The flip side of the coin is that the military overall is more fair than unfair.

Chaplains are great observers, and watching the Iraqi war unfold has truly been tough for me. I understand what the chaplains are going through; the parallels to Vietnam are excruciating to see. It makes me feel helpless, but one thing that's helped has been keeping in touch with my brother retired chaplains. For the last several years, I've been part of a chaplain e-mail group. They are terrific guys. We all served together in the military and our debates have helped me to refine my ideas toward this war from the very beginning. They've been my sounding board. Thanks to Lamar, Bernie, Clyde, Dave, Claude, Don, Charlie, and Marv.

• • •

What follows here is but a small sampling of the hundreds—perhaps thousands—of short essays I've written over the last several years. These pieces, which I affectionately call my rantings, are included in this book more because I need to express myself than because you need to read them. Most of them are a response to something that was happening to me or happening in the world, and sometimes I've included dates. I'm a hopeless news junkie and can become obsessive about the war at times. When all is said and done, my comments are just opinions. Thanks.

## Supporting the Troops

I see "Support Our Troops" ribbons everywhere. The other day, I saw two types—one yellow and one red, white, and blue. I am always grateful that Americans are supporting the troops. This support is one of the legacies of the Vietnam vet—maybe the best one. Vietnam vets were treated shabbily when they came home, and the collective American conscience now wants to make sure that the brave young Americans fighting in Iraq and Afghanistan are not similarly insulted.

Supporting the troops does not necessarily mean supporting the war. In an ideal world, an Army wouldn't be needed, but as long as we don't live in utopia, the soldier is a fact of life. Supporting the troops is not a political statement: it simply means we support the troops in war and in peace, and we owe this to them. They are in harm's way because their government, and that means all of us, sent them there.

Soldiers who die in war represent all Americans. Supporters of the war, along with those who oppose it, have an obligation to join with those on the front lines in some form of sacrifice. *The soldiers facing death daily are not players on a favorite football team. They deserve more than our cheers. They deserve our sacrifice and support.*

*May 2003*

## We Can't Leave and We Can't Stay

Supporters and critics of the war realize that this country is in a mess in Iraq. The debate is on. A National Public Radio (NPR) interviewer spoke with an artillery NCO and asked, "What are we doing in Iraq?"

The NCO answered in frustration that he had not been trained to do what he is expected to do. He was trained to fire artillery at enemy coordinates. Now he is expected to talk to the people of Iraq and to settle disputes, but he does not speak the language.

The same reporter spoke with a chaplain who seconded the NCO's remarks but added that the flip side of the coin was that the troops were bored and spent their time watching their favorite movie, *Groundhog Day,* in which Bill Murray, cast as a joke of a weather forecaster, is doomed to repeat every day again and again. Nothing changes, nothing gets better.

The war planners appear not to have taken into account two critical pieces of planning. One is that the overwhelming odds against achieving a true peace in the Middle East when Islamic fundamentalists do not promote peace with infidels. The other is that securing the country in early 2003 would have been a first step, but doing so *after* a victory will be far more difficult.

I hear that many military families either were not prepared for what lay ahead for them as their loved ones were deployed to Iraq or chose not to hear it. War is not a day at the beach—it is grim and dirty and unpredictable under the best of circumstances. Families are distraught. The Pentagon policy wonks who trumpeted that the Iraqis were going to welcome troops with open arms are dumber than I thought. Misinformation abounds.

*May 2003*

## This Is Our Leader

The following quotation is from one of the secretary of defense's briefings to the press. When one considers that he is viewed as the prime architect of the Iraq war, it becomes easier to understand how we got into such a mess.

As we know, there are known knowns. There are things we know we know. We also know there are known unknowns. That is to say, we know there are some things we do not know. But there are also unknown unknowns—the ones we don't know we don't know.

It's the same picture of some person walking out of a building with a vase and you see it 20 times and you think my goodness, were there that many vases? Is it possible that there are that many vases in the whole country?

Things will not be necessarily continuous. The fact that they are something other than ought not to

be characterizes a pause. There will be some things
that people will see. There will be some things that
people won't see. And life goes on. I think what you'll
find, I think what you'll find is, whatever it is we do
substantively, there will be near perfect clarity as to what
it is. And it will be known, and it will be known to you.

—*From a Donald Rumsfeld news briefing, February 12, 2002*

## Hollywooding the War

News organizations want to report the war; that's their
job. People at home want to hear about what's going on
with our troops. But somehow, there is something almost
profane in Hollywooding the war. Some of the material
offered from the embedded reporters during the initial
part of the Iraq war was good, but the reporters made it
"slick"—good publicity and a good story. War is not pretty
and it is not slick. *War is not a Hollywood action movie; there
are no movie trailers for the real thing.*

Hollywooding the war trivializes it. Shortly after his
capture, Saddam was paraded in front of the cameras of
news agencies. This made the country and the military
look bad—almost like gloating, which doesn't help
America's image. What punishment could possibly be
enough for this man? The fact that he didn't resist capture
and that we had to take him prisoner makes me consider
the possibilities had he resisted.

At one point in the war, a reporter took a photo in a
mosque of a young Marine who, surrounded by enemy
combatants, fired at one combatant who appeared
unarmed. We don't know enough about his situation;
the picture doesn't tell it all. The Marines were in an

impossible situation. Iraq has morphed into an impossible urban guerilla war where no one can tell the good guys from the bad. Merely to take a picture and speculate about it puts brave soldiers in critical danger.

What about the next time an enemy soldier appears to be unarmed when, in fact, he is really a dangerous combatant? This is no game. The very first American killed in Afghanistan was killed by someone he thought was unarmed. Hollywooding the war while young men and women are dying every day is disrespectful. God help us.

*December 2005*

## The Dover Test and Iraq

To Americans who care, war must be so necessary that it is in a measure acceptable in comparison to its sacrifices. In the case of Iraq, we must consider it necessary to go there to fight the war on terrorism. In my view, the sacrifices of war must pass the Dover Test. Dover is the military morgue, and I visited it during the Vietnam War.

I was escorting the body of a soldier who had been in my unit to his home. The commander felt that I needed a break from the war, and this soldier's brother had also been killed in Vietnam. There was a rule that could have gotten the second brother out of Vietnam, but that hadn't happened. While processing the paperwork and getting the soldier released to me for his final ride home, I walked into a long building thinking it was the administration building, but it was actually the morgue. The bodies of scores of American soldiers lay in long rows—soldiers who had given everything for their country. I was overwhelmed with grief.

Caring Americans need to feel that soldiers coming home to Dover have not died in vain. If they don't believe this, we'll all be questioning our presence in Iraq, as I now do. My fear is that those fine young Americans who have paid the supreme price have given their lives in vain, and Iraq is Vietnam revisited. *Can anyone in authority define "victory" for the wars in Iraq and Afghanistan?*

*December 2003*

AMERICAN MILITARY CASUALTIES IN IRAQ:
CLOSING IN ON 3000 IN MAY 2006.

## Iraqnam—No Exit Strategy

If Iraq isn't Vietnam revisited, it's darn close. In the beginning, the Vietnam war was retaliation for the Gulf of Tonkin incident. We wanted to stop communism, prevent the domino effect, flex our muscles, let a president make a splash for leadership; with a hint of morality, we could keep a big country from overrunning a small one.

In the Vietnam War, the "goal" was to win the hearts and minds of the people, and one way was through Vietnamization—training the South Vietnamese and then turning the war over to them. What's happening in Iraq sounds eerily familiar to me.

During the Vietnam war, we'd take ground one day, and give it up the next, but the Vietcong owned the night. Suddenly—to all except those fighting the war—ten years had passed and we were still fighting. And the Vietcong still owned the night. Is this what we want in Iraq?

We are at a point in Iraq where we cannot control what is going to happen. Retired generals, think-tank icons, and talk show guests and hosts all weigh in with opinion—they postulate and speculate and yet don't really know any more than the average caring American.

Military power alone can't hack it in Iraq; the forces allied against us are simply too powerful. How can any civilized nation deal with people who blow themselves up and kill innocents without a thought? Considering the thousands of years of strife in Iraq and the overlay of religiosity embedded in the souls of the people, to say nothing of our inability to fathom their history and thought processes, continuing the war indefinitely without a workable plan is sheer idiocy.

As one who has not opposed the war but who has opposed its colossal mismanagement from the beginning, I believe that an exit strategy is the way to honor our fallen soldiers and those who will die before we finally come to our senses.

*January 2004*

## Post-Traumatic Stress Disorder (PTSD) and Urban Fighting in Iraq

American soldiers in Iraq will come home with the same problems as Vietnam vets—maybe even more. No one can witness carnage and constantly be on edge without it affecting his or her psyche. I hope and pray that we've thought about reentry: helping soldiers and families prepare for going back to "normal" life.

The good news is that present-day vets will not have to fight the war at home as Vietnam vets did, which will make reentry much better for them. *Vietnam at least taught us that lesson.*

We honor soldiers who fall in battle, but how do we treat those who fight and return? At present, the majority of the country still supports soldiers, so now is the time to think about their future. If our government's past record is any indication, veterans of the Iraq war will be shortchanged. The government's sorry record on this issue goes back to World War I, when veterans couldn't even get their promised war bonuses.

The Veterans' Administration (VA), which was set up to aid vets, sometimes does the opposite. To claim what's been promised to them, vets have to go through a maze of paperwork and administrative delays. Vietnam vets had to fight to have the VA recognize PTSD and illnesses caused by Agent Orange. How many veterans died before they got their due from their country? VA funding has been cut to help absorb present war costs while our Congress approves funds to build bridges to nowhere and satisfy a host of lobbyists' demands. However, to be fair, the medical side of the VA has improved immensely and rivals any medical organization in our country. Kudos to them.

History will not call Vietnam veterans "the greatest generation" and surely will not remember the Korean War veterans. Being a vet is currently somewhat in vogue, but this may fade quickly. For the men and women who see the killing and stench of death in Iraq, uncertainty about what they will face when they come home looms ahead. After months or years fighting an urban war and dealing with the horrors of improvised explosive devices (IEDs), their futures could be almost as nightmarish as the war is.

Will they be discharged to the streets within 48 hours of returning home, as some Vietnam veterans were? Will they be sent to another military post, perhaps overseas, to finish their tour of duty, and have no reentry program there either? To give the Pentagon planners some credit, it appears that with active duty soldiers, they have learned some lessons from Vietnam regarding reentry. In this war, regular army units return together (members of the 101st Airborne return together to Fort Campbell, Kentucky, for example) and not individually. From what I read, however, this has not been the case with the Army Reserve or National Guard. We need to resolve that issue. *If more members of Congress were veterans, and if more of them had sons and daughters involved in the conflicts in Iraq and Afghanistan, maybe they would become personally invested in the well-being of veterans.*

*January 2004*

## God Is Our Refuge and Strength...

...Always ready to help in times of trouble...
Be not afraid...The Lord Almighty is with us.
He is our refuge. PSALMS 46

I was saddened while writing this book to hear of a youngster killed in Afghanistan from the small farming community where I had been pastor for several years. Many of the people who live in the town of about 5,000 knew the young man, and the town as a whole will be somewhat changed forever because of his death.

I thought of the military's process of dealing with the death of a soldier, one I participated in countless times during Vietnam. The trooper's family will be assigned a survivor assistance officer (SAO) to assist in any way possible with paperwork, benefits, and burial.

The family will enter a time of enormous grief when it is informed of the death and will grieve anew when the body comes home. Depending on the severity of the wounds, there may be viewings, with the young trooper most likely in uniform. There may be a wake, and the community will respond with grief at the funeral, which will conclude with the military's final good-bye—volleys of gunfire and the playing of taps. For those present, the scene will be overpowering—the war in Iraq will have come home to this little pocket of patriotism.

This scene has been played out in communities all across America several thousand times. The individual grief is multiplied by fathers, mothers, family members, the community. It becomes part of the community's psyche and is extremely personal. Unfortunately, it is only the beginning.

## Professional Soldiers Spend Their Careers Training for War

Someone at the Army War College in Pennsylvania produced a paper more than 20 years ago that recounted ethical problems the Army was seeing among military officers—and this was during peacetime. The issue discussed was sacrificing "duty, honor and country" on the altar of climbing the success ladder, which means making rank and getting the good assignments.

Reading the article recently started me thinking of other problems confronted by the military. There are predictions, for instance, of a large exodus from the military because soldiers have been given repeat tours to Iraq, Afghanistan, Bosnia and other hot spots around the world. Superficially, this makes sense—they're away from their families, making sacrifices—and yet a soldier trains to go to war; it is what he wants to do and what he waits for, especially if he is a professional soldier.

Training is one thing, but war gives the troops a chance to practice what they have learned—their craft. Professional soldiers want to be where the action is, and the action is at war in Iraq and Afghanistan. Even a guy like me, over the hill, still wants to get in it. When you're in the action, the problems of peacetime (backbiting, trying to get ahead and looking out for number one, reductions in force and selective early retirement) almost cease to exist and the military can do what it does best: make war.

A professional soldier rarely confesses that he loves it. He can't tell his wife that he is enjoying himself doing what he has trained for—that finally he's in the "arena" and he's feeling the adrenalin. Wives don't want to hear about it and, for that matter, neither do most Americans. War is dirty and bloody, and civilians don't want to hear that some troops look forward to doing their job.

It was years after Vietnam that I came to realize that I loved it. Where else could a person who wants to serve—a minister—have a better chance to give of himself than at war? It doesn't minimize the trauma or the horror, but it is an aspect of war that is best faced.

## The Real World and the Generals

So often, when watching C-SPAN congressional hearings about the war or military matters, I smile at the cookie-cutter image as parades of generals testify. Since so many members of congress have no military experience, they are gullible and sometimes don't ask good questions of the generals.

Congressional members may or may not grasp that when they interview a general, they are talking with another politician just like themselves. A military man does not rise to the rank of general without becoming part politician: he will have sponsors, people interested in advancing his career, and, hopefully, other qualities that make him a good leader.

I'm not really sure that questioning generals before congressional committees is the best way to get answers. There's a type of incest that occurs at the top level of the military that may not be best for the country. This is not meant to detract from the great service of our generals, but it is wise to remember that at one time, they were lieutenants. They worked hard and made their way up the chain of command and now are at the top. I hope they haven't forgotten what it was like when they led a platoon.

In my experience, the best military officers rarely make it to the top for lots of reasons. So many of the best either retire or quit early, mainly because they are uninterested in playing politics. Congress would get a better picture of the true facts in Iraq if they heard less from generals and more from lieutenants.

*April 2004*

## The Generals and Their Credibility

Skepticism is the key word. When the president says that he has given the commanders in the field what they want, what does that mean? In that scenario, it means that the commander says he doesn't need any more troops. For him to need more troops or anything else means that he is not doing his job.

An assessment of the real needs should come from the outside, not the inside. The generals have a mentality. They are four star generals; they have nowhere else to go. Would we like them to say, "We're in a mess in Iraq, we're not leaving and we need to change our course"? Or, "If it were up to me, after the constitution was ratified, I'd be out of there. We got rid of Saddam and gave you a constitution. God bless you."

It is not in the personality of generals to say either of these things. Their mentality is to please the boss and do what they're told. Most generals have come up through a system where ambition takes top billing. They are good men, but after they become generals, they also become political—as political as any politician. They may not know what the truth is or what they really believe. In order to climb up the military ladder, they have put their original thoughts and ideas on hold in the mistaken belief that once they're generals, they'll be able to resurrect some of their ideas and put them into practice.

Unfortunately, that doesn't happen. There is no way to look at Iraq in a positive way. It is a mess! We have to figure out how to extract ourselves or how to manage our involvement for a long time with minimum loss of American lives. Sadly, the generals aren't helping; in a sense, they are responsible for perpetrating a rosy picture of the situation that only makes it worse and delays the hard questions that must be asked if we are ever to see any resolution.

## Everybody in Vietnam and Iraq Is in Somebody's Army

It was one thing when soldiers were moving into Baghdad with tanks and fire support, but now they're out there daily, totally vulnerable in a guerrilla war. Life is different when you're trying to figure out who the innocents are.

Soldiers in Iraq are involved in the worst kind of combat—an urban guerrilla war. Our war in Vietnam was different. We actually saw more combat than the soldiers in Iraq are seeing—by most accounts, 200 days of combat a year—but when we encountered civilians, it was not in large urban areas, where chaos is more the rule than the exception. Innocent civilians are dying by the score in Iraq every day.

Nebraska's Bob Kerry once discussed on television a statement he made about the killing of innocent civilians in Vietnam. He said the reason he was making the statement publicly was that one of the members of his Navy Seal team had lied when he said that innocent civilians were lined up and killed. Kerry said what really happened during that particular operation was that his group took fire from a village, and they fired back. Kerry's view was that the innocents were killed in crossfire. Once the Americans entered the village, they discovered ten or twelve dead civilians: women and children. I believe him.

We know that innocents were killed occasionally in Vietnam, but probably there was VC activity, too. (We surely remember My Lai, an awful and tragic aberration.) Kerry said the civilians were not indiscriminately lined up and shot; it did not happen that way. Many Vietnam and Iraq war combat veterans have been in the same situation. Everybody in the country appears to be in somebody's army. As Kerry said in a later interview, the problem was the war, not the soldier.

Sadly, a guerilla war, by its very nature, causes civilian casualties, no matter what war.

## Enraged

While writing this book, I read that a father had become enraged over the death of his son, a young soldier killed in Iraq in his own mess hall. I see "enraged" as a appropriate word to describe his feelings. Losing a son or daughter at war under any condition should make one enraged. However, the mess hall suicide bombing that took this young man's life touched a nerve—it was intolerable and makes evident the politics of war.

Is there anyplace that an American soldier in Iraq should feel comfortable or safe? No, this is war. But one would think that the place most likely to be safe probably would be the mess hall, where soldiers are eating, laughing, joking, taking a break. To have that small illusion of comfort taken away through the fanaticism of a suicide bomber is truly a reason to be enraged.

Is what happened anybody's fault (other than the bomber's)? No, not really, when you consider the environment; but the lesson learned is that no one can be trusted in this very painful war. Americans are attempting to engage the Iraqis in their own country's fight. They are training policemen, soldiers and security people. The soldiers are being told to be friendly, to talk to Iraqis, to befriend them, and they are doing it. In this case, they were blown up for doing just that. (We now have evidence that some of our soldiers may have been killed by Iraqis they were training to be soldiers.)

So, what can soldiers do? Policies will change: flak vests will be worn to chow, and every kind of precaution will be taken, but total protection can never happen. Fanatics are willing to kill and be killed in senseless ways. Fanaticism is a mentality that defies logic, and we need to call it what it is. Muslim fanatics bent on killing Americans seem just as happy to kill their own people. It is what makes this war insane and not winnable. It is what enrages us in our grief. Soldiers are not "safe" anywhere. Muslim fundamentalists have declared a holy war on America because we are not "believers." We are infidels to them and must be converted to Islam or die.

*January 2004*

## Chaplain Yee

Of all the sorry stories about our misadventures into the realm of terrorism, the story of Chaplain Yee is the most disturbing and frightening to me. A Muslim chaplain who is a West Point graduate and was a captain in the United States Army, he was accused of having unauthorized documents and of aiding the prisoners at Guantanamo. Most disturbing was the fact that other chaplains and professionals in the Army didn't support him in any way that I know. He was blindfolded and placed in shackles, and he languished in jail, in solitary confinement, for 76 days.

All charges were eventually dropped, and the flimsiest excuses were given for ever having filed them in the first place. The powers that be used no common sense, and I believe that this sort of idiocy is more self-defeating than anything else. We charge people with little evidence, hold them for long periods without justification, and ignore what is happening to them. All of this is done, supposedly, to fight terrorism.

Yee's military career is over. He received what is commonly called a "letter of reprimand," which he appealed. The reprimand was thrown out—the only smart thing the Army appears to have done in this case.

We probably shouldn't even have Muslim chaplains in the military. We could handle chaplain coverage by contract with a Muslim clergy group to minister to Muslims. Unfortunately, the chief of chaplains at the time was so eager to jump on the bandwagon of PC (political correctness) that he broke a tradition older than the country—recognizing three major faith groups: Protestant, Catholic, and Jewish.

It was later discovered that Yee was not as pure as the driven snow—he supposely had a sexual liaison with a female lieutenant at Guantanamo, for which he was later charged. Adultery, while emotionally detrimental to all those involved when it becomes public, is rarely prosecuted in the military. If the transgression affects good order and discipline or is disruptive, then maybe something is done. I don't mean to downplay what Captain Yee did or didn't do, but apparently the affair was secret until the Army tried to conjure something up.

The disturbing things about Captain Yee's situation were how trumped up it all appeared to be, how little support he received from those who should have been making sure justice was done, and that nobody who treated him badly had to own up to it.

## The Psyche of the Soldier

National Public Radio (NPR) produced a program some time ago on the aftermath of the Iraq war and brought in a couple of college professors as "experts." The program focused on emotional issues for combat soldiers as a result of the Iraq War. One of the experts lamented that a full 10 percent of the military evacuees from Iraq left the war for emotional or psychological reasons. I verified this information later when talking with a nurse major who regularly flew from Germany to Kuwait to evacuate soldiers wounded in action.

We are fighting the absolutely worst kind of war: an urban guerilla war where it is close to impossible to distinguish the good guys from the bad ones—those previously described fanatics who can kill their own people.

The NPR experts sounded inadequate to me—a little over their heads. One even mentioned that many American soldiers coming home from Iraq will have to deal with the fact that they have murdered someone.

Whoa! No soldier in the act of war "murders" anyone. Murder implies criminal activity or premeditation. Killing is an act of war. It is part of war, and the soldier may have to deal with it emotionally, but murder is assuredly not the correct term. Kill or be killed is the concept—not murder.

We watch the news reports: the killings, the beheadings, throat-slittings, bombings. We sit in the comfort of our homes and watch gruesome reality. The combat soldier does not have that luxury. He lives the nightmare.

The loss of life in war is an act of war, nothing else. I'm not arguing semantics here; soldiers at war do not go to war on their own. Their country sends them. Their service is a commitment to go bravely against an enemy in the act of war.

The American cause is the cause of freedom for soldiers. Soldiers must believe their cause is worthy and just. Their belief is part of their psyche. Emotionally, soldiers must believe in the course of action their country has taken. They are not involved in politics or propagating a way of life, surely not in Iraq. In their minds and hearts, soldiers' causes are just and honorable. May God bless each and every soldier and bring them safely home.

## Fallen Soldiers

Early in the war, the *San Francisco Chronicle* carried the pictures of all the troops killed in Iraq by that time. Looking at those young faces is heartbreaking. What war does to you—among many things—is make you hate it. Robert E. Lee was supposed to have said, "It is well that war is so terrible, or we should grow too fond of it." I agree.

What so squeezes the heart is that these kids never got to live out their lives. We old soldiers have lived ours. Most combat Vietnam veterans are living on borrowed time anyway. I've done most of the things I want to do, but these kids won't have a chance. The fallen soldiers are real people with real moms, dads, brothers, sisters, husbands, wives, sweethearts, cousins. It would be amazing to follow the connections to see how many the loss of one person touches. Some may say that compared to other wars, the losses in this war don't amount to much. But for the individual, the pain is 100 percent.

*March 2004*

## Has 9/11 Really Changed Us?

I wish I could say yes, but "not really" is the answer. Each 9/11 anniversary week, we have a media blitz, but most of the media have it wrong. Television stations have time slots to fill, and the programmers fill them with a perception that has little resemblance to reality.

*September 11 did change us for the moment, but not permanently overall as a nation.* Think about it: most of the sacrifices being made by Americans are by soldiers at war. The rest of the country appears to have returned quickly to business as usual. For the victims and families and for people in the geographical areas of New York and Washington, D.C., maybe there's been some change. Certainly, we've changed on the security front, and life has definitely changed for Arab Americans.

Politicians are fond of using the phrase "the American people." They need to qualify that concept. How about American people *who care?* The late Walt Rostow had it right—he was referring to politics but it fits—when he said that *a politician must get 60 percent of the people for him. Twenty-five percent will be against everything, and 15 percent are out to lunch.* Let's face it, most Americans are not truly engaged unless they have some personal investment in a situation. Currently, there is no shared sacrifice.

September 11 gave us a great chance to make changes, but we let it slip away. We had a chance to encourage our young people to serve their country. Congress could have enacted a two-year required universal service for our young people. Politics would have been involved, but they could have done it. Americans who have any interest are still too ready to let someone else's children fight their wars.

*So—did September 11 affect us?* Yes, for a time: Church attendance was up, military recruiters had kids ready to sign up; the timing was there. But then the window closed and we're back to business as usual.

*Terrorism is not going to be eradicated.* Terrorism, unlike the Vietnam war or various other crises, is not going away. As long as people are as fanatical about killing us as Osama and his gang are, terrorism will be with us. My sad prediction is that the hatred, fueled mainly by the Mideast, will go on and on, and we have to live with it. There will be other 9/11s and our hope is that we will rise to the occasion as a nation and not collapse in a heap of self-interest as we did after September 11, 2001.

*September 11, 2002*

## Casualty of War

Many tragedies happen in war and we understand them. However, I'm not sure that there is any greater tragedy than what can happen to the psyches of soldiers. A mentality seems to develop if people are put in the same stressful situation often enough, whether it's combat or being a guard at the Guantanamo Bay prison.

I read once that in prisons in general, after a while it becomes difficult to know who the guards are and who the prisoners are. Meaning, of course, that the guards often come across as unfeeling and uncaring and may exhibit bad behavior, as the guards did at Abu Ghraib. We may even see extreme situations like the five soldiers accused recently of raping and killing an Iraqui teenager. We ask ourselves how this could happen. What is this mentality that war has created?

All along the idea of the Guantanamo prison has seemed insane to me. Why would we hold a bunch of mostly low-level terrorists in a prison, subjecting ourselves to worldwide criticism? Surely, there's nothing they can tell us that we don't already know. The argument that putting them back into circulation will enable them to fight another day simply doesn't make sense—there's no shortage of terrorists. They multiply daily. It has often appeared to me that the Guantanamo situation is like the war in Iraq: here we are, we made a stupid mistake but now we don't know how to get out of it so we perpetuate the same mistake.

We have always prided ourselves on treating people right—following the Golden Rule even under awful circumstances. We would never do as the Germans did in World War II; we'd surely not be as cruel as the Japanese were to our POWs; and we'd never treat downed pilots the way North Vietnam did ours. It is not in our nature.

Yet at Guatanamo Bay prison, we have reduced ourselves to the lowest mentality. When the final line has been written about the aftermath of 9/11 and our own feelings of insecurity, Guantanamo may be the most questioned spectacle of all.

Issues of right and wrong have an effect on American soldiers who deal with Guantanamo prisoners day after day. Treating people badly gets into their psyche and they and us by extension are much the worse for it. Closing this prison and others like it is long overdue. It is a sorry situation, and the young Americans who have served there will pay for it for a long time. God bless them and us.

## Proud of This Soldier

Recently, I had dinner with an old buddy who is now a colonel stationed at the Pentagon. I was eager to talk with him about Iraq, but it was tough drawing anything out of him. He seemed naïve about the war in some ways and knowledgeable in others. He seemed to be singing the administration's song—the news media is creating a distorted, negative picture of the war and that on the contrary, we're doing a lot of good by setting up orphanages and schools and most Iraqis want us there. Some of this may be true; the media does go for sensation and what's happening *now*: suicide and roadside bombings, torture killings, kidnappings, sectarian violence running rampant.

Still, I did come away from the conversation with a smidgen of hope. Despite the current situation in Iraq, I was hopeful and full of pride to see this soldier, whom I saw come through the ranks, have such passion and enthusiasm for the military and its missions. I had brought him into the Army as a green lieutenant and helped him start a great career. He was fresh from ROTC, very naïve, and somewhat unsure about even being in the military. I remember saying to him once when he was lamenting that the military was not quite what he expected: "Lieutenant, what did you think this would be? Summer camp?"

He was within a hair of being swallowed up in the bureaucracy of the Army at Fort Bragg, North Carolina. We stole him and entrenched him in the 82$^d$ Airborne Division before anybody knew it. Then we sent him to jump school and made him into a paratrooper, and suddenly this nonmacho shy lieutenant was gung-ho. Today he's a colonel and doing a good job and encouraging me to keep the faith about Iraq. Not a bad thing.

*July 2004*

## Modern Day Soldiering Among a Disinterested Public

A modern-day airport is a great place to people-watch. These days I watch with a sense of poignancy because there are always a few uniformed soldiers sitting and waiting. This is a change from soldiering during Vietnam. For one thing, in the latter days of Vietnam, we were not allowed to travel in uniform lest someone discover we were soldiers. In the early days of the war, when soldiers returned from the Nam, they were proud. Regardless of what anyone else thought, they had been serving their country, and they were proud soldiers. Their traveling uniform was khakis and brightly colored badges and hero medals. But it didn't take long for that situation to end: soon came the protests, various negative incidents, and the Vietnam soldier being blamed for the war.

In an airport recently, I watched a young couple for about an hour off and on. Her eyes were swollen from crying. I thought, *What is their story? How are their finances? Do they live in government housing? What sort of support will she have while her husband is off at war? If he is killed, what protection will she have for the future?* The questions are endless. They had a small daughter who will be without her daddy for a year—maybe forever.

It is war. Combat soldiers are trained for war, but their families also have to endure the separation—the times when Daddy or Mommy is absent from events like birthdays, school plays, and various family crises. These are unbelievably sacrificial times. Hard, hard times. The general public doesn't appreciate what soldiers and their families go through—mainly, I hope, because they don't understand it. Very few Americans have served in the military; it's not an option they ever considered. Many in our culture are proud that their grandfathers and great grandfathers served, but being in the service is foreign to most people, and this is very sad for our culture.

*December 2004*

## Have We Forgotten to Say Thanks?

Recently, on a Delta flight, I saw a first sergeant on the plane. He was dressed in his BDUs (battle dress uniform), obviously just back from Iraq. I always hesitate to talk to soldiers because I don't want to give them the third degree. He looked very tired and I wondered where he might be going. I discovered he was on the way home for emergency leave; his wife had suffered complications during pregnancy. He didn't go into it too much and I didn't press. I briefly said how much I appreciated his service and commitment. He said thanks and that was it.

I observed for a couple of hours, and I was the only one who spoke with him during that time. I wondered about all those feel-good stories I'd seen on the Internet: the soldier gets on the plane, the passengers give him a spontaneous round of applause and then proceed to ply him with drinks and food—in other words, folks rewarding soldiers for their great service.

I'm beginning to think that the stories are made up; they either didn't happen or folks feel differently about soldiers than they did three years ago. In the beginning of the Iraq war, most folks were supportive and always supported the troops, whatever that might mean. But Americans don't have a long attention span—something is on their radar screen and they respond, then it passes and they're on to the next event.

I fear that folks are not focused on the war anymore. Young Americans are dying daily, but somehow we are not distressed about it. It is business as usual. I don't want it to be that way. I want all of us to suffer somewhat. But without a military draft and most of the population not having had any military experience—and not even *knowing* anyone who has had military experience, we are not collectively grieving. We are not hurting. I hope I'm wrong but fear that I'm not.

It was good to see the young troop in his desert uniform; maybe the uniform caught someone's eye. I'm glad to see soldiers traveling in their work uniforms. They are fighting a war—and, it does remind me of a war story.

I was a young captain during the sixties in Washington D. C. for the March on the Pentagon. My unit stayed after the march. We were camped in tents at the National Park Service Headquarters. It was Easter, and I took a group of soldiers—there were a couple of dozen of us—to a fancy Masonic outdoor amphitheater for an Easter sunrise service. We were in our fatigues (our work uniforms). A well-dressed gentleman arrived on the scene and asked us to leave—we weren't properly dressed. We were only soldiers in our work clothes protecting these people! When I voiced my objections not too calmly, he said we could stay if we moved to the back of the crowd. We did and I've never forgotten it.

Now it is not as bad as it was then. Maybe we have made progress. One of the legacies of the Vietnam war is that the soldiers were treated so shabbily that the country, over more than 30 years, has felt a collective shame. Now, thankfully, most people realize soldiers are just doing their jobs. At least for that, we are grateful.

*April 2006*

## The Chain of Command

I can't remember anything that has disturbed me more than the recent allegations of rape and murder against our troops in Iraq. If the allegations are true, my first question is: where was the chain of command?

The military is built around the chain of command. What that means is that every soldier has someone in charge of him or her. Those soldiers sitting at a checkpoint outside the Iraqi village of Mahmoudiya had a fire team leader who was the highest ranking person over their five-man team. The fire team leader had a squad leader who had a platoon sergeant who had a platoon leader (an officer) who had a company commander. These are the very basics of the chain of command. No soldier operates in isolation.

When we hear of incidents like this or Abu Ghraib, the first question to be asked is, *Where was the chain of command?*

*July 2006*

# Psychobabbling Crime

The recently discharged soldier accused of masterminding a heinous rape in Iraq has a personality disorder, or so says the military, which used this reason for kicking him out. A delusional loner who can't take criticism, blames others, hates authority, and takes orders from God. This could be any number of people in government. If he is guilty—and given the military's penchant for covering its posterior, he probably is, along with other soldiers—as an ex-soldier, I am heartsick. His actions were premeditated—or so say the experts—and this could mean the death penalty.

I like to put our troops on a pedestal, but I know there are bad apples throughout society, and some of them make it into the military. The accused soldier was a train wreck waiting to happen. How do people like him get into the military? Most are youngsters who have messed up but deserve another chance, and they find it in the military.

I have long advocated that the military be a rehabilitative society for kids on the fringes. Why not? It has doctors, lawyers, chaplains, social workers—a system that works. Potential soldiers get waivers for all sorts of things: pot busts, misdemeanors of certain kinds, and an occasional felony. We can take some social misfits and make them into contributing soldiers. Success happens more often than not.

It is easy to condemn the entire process, but no way! Outside of the guilty parties in the rape case, if there is a culprit, it is a breakdown of the military's chain of command. The reason we do better than our civilian counterparts at policing potentially trouble-causing soldiers is that we have a system designed to prevent them from being stupid or criminal. It is broadly called *leadership* and specifically called the *chain of command*. In this case the chain of command broke down.

It is true that the Army needed recruits, but the troubled enlistees make up a small part, maybe 5 to 15 percent. This accused malefactor represents one of those cases that fits well with psychobabble—combat-stressed with at least seventeen members of his battalion killed, two of them mutilated after being kidnapped. Eight of the total were part of his company (a hundred men or so).

The accused soldier's family, according to news reports, wasn't exactly a paragon of stability. Somehow he managed to get a GED, and up until the incident in Iraq, his brushes with the law were not earth-shattering (one, for example, was for possession of tobacco). How did this troubled individual make it as far as he did in the military? Basic and advanced individual training should have been enough to weed him out. Even though basic training is probably not as hard as it was in the old days, it's still no cakewalk.

The guy, if we believe what we read, has a significant disabling and dangerous condition—possibly paranoid and beset by anxieties and delusional fears. If he committed a crime, he had a habitual pattern of lying and ignoring the suffering of others. Did this disturbed individual's disorder help him to masquerade as a bold, effective 11 Bravo (infantryman)? A soldier like the accused might have some charisma—some surface traits that appear to make him a good soldier. And it sounds like as a ringleader, he manipulated those who should have stopped the crime cold, including two sergeants (those men are supposed to be leaders—that's why they're sergeants).

Assuming this soldier was a nut case, the Army got him out, but too late. In reality, there's no way to stop 100 percent of the nuts. Some will slip through the cracks. Rehabilitation doesn't happen, because they're sick and possibly beyond cure—all the more reason we need vigilant leaders.

This is such a tragic story in many ways, most of all for the poor Iraqi family. They are not the cost of war, rather the victims of insanity.

*July 2006*

## It is Immoral for Other People's Children to Fight Our Wars

Universal service is more than a worthy idea. The odds are strongly against our country having a military draft ever again. Even the Republican platform of the last election said "no" to the draft. We had a sham of a vote in congress on the draft. Congressman Charles Rangel of New York sponsored two bills (in 2003 and 2005) calling for the reinstatement of the draft, mainly with the motivation of making a statement. He said, and I agree, that it is totally unfair to have a small segment of society—the volunteer army—bear the burden for the country's wars. Rangel primarily is talking about minorities. I would take it several steps further. It is morally reprehensible to have the most vulnerable of our society act as our surrogates in war.

One congressman went so far as to say that we should hire mercenaries—that we don't want our young boys and girls fighting our wars. I could hardly believe my ears, and it made me ashamed.

During the last election, part of the "hit" pieces concerning candidates consistently used the possibility of the draft to denounce candidates. What those who developed this "no military draft" e-mail campaign don't get is that a form of the draft would accomplish their goals. How? One of the things America should be about is serving the country, giving back for all the great benefits that the country has given us. If we had a type of universal service in which all had to serve—no exceptions—political leadership would be reluctant to commit us to war. With the present war in Iraq, the president did not have to pay a political price for his decisions. Why? Few people of influence were personally involved, as they had no son or daughter serving. The military draft only became a footnote issue because of the election.

The all-volunteer Army is composed of mostly working-class kids who probably have few options. This doesn't mean that we don't have a highly trained and dedicated military. We do. What this *does* mean is that the military is not representative of our society, and this is wrong.

## Universal Service

For some time, I have been concerned about our *fractured culture*. Recently, *Reader's Digest* had an article about whether we are truly a "fractured America." It concluded "not as much as we think," but unfortunately, we let the left and right drive us, according to the article. I'm not so sure. I would like to think that most of us congregate in the middle, but I have my doubts.

I hate labels. Who can call someone conservative, liberal, far right, left-leaning? I would view myself as a thinking American, independent.

The result of the last presidential election is credited to the right-wing fundamentalists of the Republican party. Assuming this to be so, they were able to do this only because a large contingent of young people, whom Democrats were counting on—simply didn't vote. To me, there's a great lesson in this: *We have to have something other than politics to unite us.* The benefits of some type of *universal service* are legion. One, above all, is the *unifying* factor. In our extremely polarized country, we need something to unify us. What better than youth, 18–26, with a common experience?

## Don't Bother Us

The third anniversary of the war in Iraq came and went without much fanfare. None of the old Vietnam-style protests (whether they did any good or not), and the few that were held didn't get much attention and few young people showed up or had any interest, it seems. Why? It's simply that kids, like most adults, don't have any vested interest in the war. It really is not affecting them. Life goes on, and youngsters don't have to worry about being drafted and so why get excited—you have a war, you have someone else doing the fighting. What's the big deal?

In some ways, it is not that activism has disappeared. According to various reports, students are getting involved in such endeavors as *Teach America*, and there's been a resurgence of interest in the Peace Corps. Many students went to help clean up and rebuild after Hurricane Katrina. Maybe it's just the idea of an abstract war going on somewhere else, not really affecting anybody other than those fighting and their families. And, of course, the political spin that the volunteer military is working out well can't be discounted. It is working only in terms of fielding a military—and a good one—but not one that's representative of America.

## Where Are the Vietvets in Support of Universal Service?

Vietnam vets in government are rare these days, but there are a few. Some didn't serve—like Vice President Dick Cheney, who has said he had "other priorities" during the war in Vietnam. But what about Vietnam vets like Senator John Kerry, John McCain, Chuck Hegel and former Secretary of State Colin Powell—Vietnam veterans who have seen young men die in combat? Don't they "get it"? Fighting a war on the backs of working-class Americans is simply not right. They know better, and the draft was a factor in Vietnam, even if it was a somewhat convoluted system. At least all men of age were duty-bound to register because of the draft. When I debate those who oppose any sort of military draft, I always say, "I have no argument and can merely say this: it is unjust and immoral for a small segment of Americans to fight such a war in Iraq." There is no other argument in my mind that has credibility.

## How About a Tour in the Marines?

I first read this in a newspaper column: *teenagers concerned over their rights*—roughly meaning that teenagers and parents are locked in a battle over teenagers' rights. What rights are those? According to the article, the teenagers *get to choose whatever those rights might be.* What is this? Kids from affluent homes need to get a life. They spend way too much time on the Internet, text messaging their friends, and focusing on themselves, and parents allow it to happen. Give me a break! When parents cede control to teenagers, the kids are going to take it. When kids don't have to face responsibilities, old fashioned things like a job, for instance, what can we expect?

In a related but more serious vein is a recent article I read: "When we let them down, kids get high"—about bored kids doing drugs. The article was written by a therapist who, in my opinion, removes the responsibility for taking drugs from the kids and places it on the adults—we're not listening to the kids. They are bored with life; their mantra is that life sucks and consequently drugs are a way to make it not so.

According to the story, many of these kids know how to score Oxycontin, a pain medication derived from opium, along with designer drugs and methamphetamines with the ease of opening a Coke can. She states, "It's happening here at beautiful _____. People come to enjoy a nice vacation, drive SUVs the size of tanks, and are unwilling to face the reality that the local ski areas would probably have very few employees if companies tested for drugs and enforced a clean and sober policy at work."

Wow! What ever happened to kids doing homework, having an after-school job, playing sports, hanging out with girlfriends or boyfriends? And, more importantly, where are the parents? Are they scared to confront their kids lest the kids become alienated? I don't want to sound judgmental, but please, give me a break.

I have a solution for the therapist who feels so strongly the plight of the teenagers she's counseling. What about the Army or Marines? What about kids knowing that at some point, bored or not, they are going to have to face the military draft or some alternative? Why not? What do we think is going to happen to many of these kids who at age eleven know how to get drugs and get high? They are going to be a burden on society at some point. Even among baby boomers today, many face health problems related to their "summers of love," and today's kids will be much worse as adults, if they make it to adulthood at all.

If we involve them in something with a purpose, they might have a chance. There should be an *AllServe*. (*AllServe* is the name I've given to my last ten years of effort to get politicians or anyone else interested in some type of universal service for young Americans). If these kids had to serve in something—the military or some sort of universal service like the Peace Corps or Americorps, they might just find purpose. Sound far-fetched? Not any more than doing nothing.

## Universal Service Will Sell

I am discovering that many Americans will go for *universal service* if youth are given an option. When I first began my campaign ten years ago, it was just about the military draft. I could count on one hand those who mildly agreed. Thinking has changed, though, and more and more parents of eligible kids see the advantage. Having a choice is the selling point. *AllServe* needs to be promoted and a formal organization created with a buildup of support in the country. Once this happens, the congress will follow.

There are so many positives to this approach. First of all, it could be phased in over ten years and promoted among our youngsters now. *Teach America* is a success story and an example of the way *AllServe* could work. They recruit top graduates who could be in medical school or Wharton or wherever—yet they choose to do something meaningful before they start their careers. *Teach America* sends graduates into poor rural and urban schools for two years. For many, it has become a next step after graduation. These kids want to contribute to improving society while keeping their options open. *Teach America* drew applications from 12 percent of the graduates at Yale, 11 percent at Dartmouth, and 8 percent at Harvard. All told, a record 17,350 applied in one year.

Are our kids ready to opt more aggressively for public service? I think so. Many of those volunteering for *Teach America* don't know what they want to do. The thought is that with the kids not knowing what to do, they should take some time to do something meaningful for a couple of years and think about the future. Military service is only one of the options. Universal service will work.

## No Incentive to Serve

Without a draft or any sort of universal service, kids don't have an incentive to serve. I talk to parents of kids of draft age and find that unless there is an unusual circumstance, they don't even think about it. In a bitterly divided country involved in a very divisive war that rational people see no end to, the vast majority agree that our troops should not be held accountable for the politics that led to Iraq becoming Iraqnam.

For most of us Vietnam vets who think about it, our great legacy is the fact that most Americans who care—and not all do—realize that soldiers who fought in Vietnam were blamed for the war—even for the lies about what we were doing in Vietnam and the mismanagement of battle plans we could not salvage. For the most part, we're determined not to make that mistake again. This time around, most of us salute our soldiers.

That being said, the vast majority of Americans are still willing for other people's kids to fight their wars. Three long years ago, when the invasion of Iraq was widely supported as an extension of the war on terror, the prospect of a military draft was occasionally mentioned, but with rancor more than anything else. Simply stated, across party lines, especially among the affluent classes, the draft was a word uttered with disdain if at all—in no way do we want our sons and daughters to serve the nation's military. Nothing has changed.

## Politics of the Draft

The politics of the draft reflected the vast majority of Americans' thoughts. The volunteer Army was touted as sufficient. Let's face it—all those hawks who supported the war and still do not have any "skin" in the game. It doesn't affect them or their families. I'm not much of a Michael Moore fan, as he's taken his antigovernment crusade to an absurd level while making a sack full of money from his movies. But there is a priceless scene in *Fahrenheit 9-11* when he approaches congressmen, wanting to give them paperwork for their sons and daughters about joining the military. Gotta love it. Congressional hypocrisy at its height: sending other moms' and dads' kids off to war.

## Who Are These Kids Who Fight for America?

They are, by and large, from America's working class. Why do they join up? Let's subscribe to them the best of motives: patriotism, which is relatively accurate. When parents or wives or friends are interviewed at their funerals, it sounds so much better to talk about their patriotism. In reality, however, they are kids whose economic prospects are less than stellar. They are high school graduates who are not going to college because of costs. Many are young parents who need a regular paycheck and health care for their families.

According to DOD statistics, the average soldier comes from a household earning between $32,000 and $33,500. (The median American income is $43,300.) There's a sense of denial in the people I talk to who are willing to admit that we've left the burden of defending an affluent nation to those who enjoy less of its affluence. It isn't so much classic denial as that they simply don't want to 'fess up. Occasionally, one of my buddies will say, "Well, they volunteered." This is true, and we have to affirm kids for doing this, but it does not alter who they are—many relate their service to 9/11 and duty, honor, country—who can argue with that? However, it does mean that the wealthier kids surely didn't get overwhelmed with patriotism.

## Why Don't Kids Join Up?

Kids don't join up for many reasons: a war, a good economy, growing resistance to the military by parents and zealots. Congress wants the Army to expand by at least 50,000 troops, yet the military is having a hard time even maintaining the status quo. Where are they going to get 50,000 more soldiers? The Army is obviously in a hurt. Afghanistan and Iraq are long-term commitments, and there seems to be no letup in either war. The powers that be give rosy descriptions, but who believes them anymore? Not anybody I know.

## Universal Service Is the Answer

In a perfect world, we would not need an army, but unless horses start to fly and the Democrats and the Republicans lie down together in the hereafter, I am beginning to see a crack in the intransigent views. Congress will not even consider a draft. When the draft issue was raised, it was merely symbolic. However, all of this is missing the boat. If we had an *AllServe* approach to universal service, the draft would be only one small aspect of the total picture. We would be limited only by our own imagination. We could have teachers corps, peace corps, domestic service corps; we could mimic programs that many states and cities already have in place. Military service would be a small portion of it.

This idea isn't radical—merely practical. Would young Americans join the military in great numbers? Maybe, but the military is really not the point. *Service* is. We've already seen the evidence during a crisis; in fact, many in our volunteer army now were recruited after 9/11. The most famous recruit, of course, is the now deceased Pat Tillman. A million-dollar NFL contract would not deter him from service. Even considering questions about how he died, nothing can detract from his sacrifices. What *AllServe* would do for many is nudge them toward what they want to do anyway. There would be no deferments.

This idea is more feasible than initiating a military draft, which may become a possibility, and we are at a point where we can give no credence to those who run the military recruiting program. They have failed, and all their pronouncements will make no difference. Our present military is woefully under-sized for the commitments we have, and we are incredibly lucky that we have not had to deal with a truly major conflict.

What if—by some stretch of the imagination—we had to take on a major power like China, with its unlimited manpower. They could easily overwhelm us, creating unthinkable options like nuclear war. Without getting into strategy, *AllServe* needs merely to think in terms of numbers. The benefits to an *AllServe* are legion. The most important is the unifying factor. I say again, in our extremely divisive country, we need something to unify us. What better than youth, 18–26, with a common experience. *AllServe* would provide such an experience.

## Salute to Chaplains Serving In Iraq

What about chaplains at war? On the one hand, it is a great opportunity to minister—the very best. Where better can a minister feel needed than at war? The opportunities are endless.

But what about the chaplain's own belief and approach to the war? Does the chaplain need to feel that the war is justified or buy into the reasons for being there? In World War II, the reasons were clear. Since then, with the possible exception of Korea, this has not held true.

The reasons for wars since Korea have been ambiguous and driven by other forces, such as politics. In the case of Iraq, the jury is out, to a large degree, with the verdict falling more and more on the side of miscalculation. The administration of this war has been a template for mismanagement. Iraq may be a "fast train to nowhere," so where does a man of God stand? Most chaplains serve because they see the need for ministry in the war zone regardless of their opinion of war, and we need to salute this attitude. In the HBO documentary *Baghdad ER*, which shows the hectic life of doctors, nurses, and chaplains in an emergency room in the Green Zone, an Army chaplain prays over a dead soldier: "Lord, you brought him to us. We tried everything we could to save his life. But it was not up to us. Lord, we pray that his life and even his death might be used to hasten peace and end this terrible war."

God bless the chaplains in Iraq and the men and women they serve.

*May 2006*

# History of the Vietvet Family Project

Not a day passes that I don't think about Vietnam. It was the pivotal time of my life—life-changing is more like it. Unlike many of those who stayed on active duty, I stayed involved with vets. For many career soldiers, Vietnam was just one more thing they went through. Not me. Since Nam, it has always been a part of my psyche. I always wanted to do something that related in one way or another to Vietnam. I felt guilt. I didn't know exactly what kind or why; it was mainly an institutional guilt: *as a country, we made all these promises and then ran off and left the people.*

After my last tour in Korea (1986–87), I corralled a few buddies and we formed a nonprofit organization called the **Vietnam Veterans Southeast Asian Children's Project**. We really didn't have a clue what we wanted to do. Part of my thinking was that there were other GIs who felt like me. We felt we owed the Vietnamese something, especially those who helped and supported us, and helping Vietnamese kids was something we could do. The idea was that we would attempt to help Vietnamese refugee kids in the United States. What we discovered quickly was that of all the immigrants who might need assistance, the Vietnamese didn't. At least in San Francisco, every Vietnamese kid had three paper routes and spoke English better than most of us did.

## A Transition

Next we came up with the idea that maybe our efforts could best be used to help Amerasian kids (kids with GI fathers and Vietnamese mothers). We found very quickly, with the few such children we contacted through the Pearl Buck Foundation and a couple of other groups, that what they wanted most was to find their fathers. But guess what? Most of the fathers didn't want to be found. Our organization became OBE (overcome by events).

A few years ago, a few of us resurrected the original nonprofit and renamed it the *Vietvets Family Project*. We wanted to keep it alive as a conduit for Vietnam vets who wanted an opportunity to give back. After 9/11, in our grief and feelings of helplessness, we were moved to do something. We raised the money for one school in Vietnam—a preschool in a little village called Hai Tan, north of Hue—with much help from my former church. We had enough money left over for a language lab in the Cholon district of Saigon. The project was actually shepherded by *Room to Read*, a wonderful nonprofit in San Francisco (www.roomtoread.org).

## Our Purpose

As funds are available, the Vietvet Family Project gives small scholarships to anyone who comes to our attention whom we can encourage. In the past couple of years, we've helped a nursing student get a computer, paid for a certification course for a kindergarten teacher, sponsored students in yoga physical education classes, and donated to vets who helped in New Orleans after Katrina.

*The Hai Tan preschool built with funds from the Vietvets Family Project.*

Cover and book design by
Sue Knopf/Graffolio
La Crosse, Wisconsin

This book was created using Adobe InDesign CS
on a Macintosh G4.

Fonts are from the Palatino, and Jacoby families.

Some graphics were created by the designer.

Printed and bound by
McNaughton & Gunn,
Saline, Michigan